The Boat

The Boat

By the Editors of
TIME-LIFE BOOKS

The

TIME-LIFE Library of Boating

TIME-LIFE BOOKS, NEW YORK

The Cover: Leaning into the turn, a 35-foot sport fisherman passes close astern of a 38-foot sailboat on the calm waters of California's Santa Monica Bay. The powerboat's skipper steers from a flying bridge, while the crew of the sailing craft cope with the taut cat's cradle of lines that control the boat's working sails.

The Consultants: Carleton Mitchell, whose introduction to *The Boat* begins on page 8, has logged more than 50 years as a racing skipper, cruising man and author.

John D. Atkin is a yacht designer and professional surveyor as well as Commodore of the Huntington Cruising Club of Darien, Connecticut.

Alan Gurney is a yacht designer whose racing sailboats, such as *Guinevere* and *Windward Passage,* have won trophies in ocean races worldwide.

G. James Lippmann, a naval architect, is the executive director of the American Boat and Yacht Council.

Conrad Miller, a technical editor of *Motor Boating & Sailing* and a consultant to the Westlawn School of Yacht Design, is author of *Small Boat Engines* and other books on marine technology.

John Rousmaniere, a small-boat sailor and veteran ocean racer, is the West Coast editor of *Yachting* magazine.

Owen C. Torrey Jr. is chief designer for Charles Ulmer, Inc., sailmakers.

Valuable assistance was given by the following departments and individuals of Time Inc.: Editorial Production, Norman Airey; Library, Benjamin Lightman, Lester Annenberg; Picture Collection, Doris O'Neil; Photographic Laboratory, George Karas; TIME-LIFE News Service, Murray J. Gart; Correspondents Jane Estes (Seattle), Margot Hapgood (London).

Contents

THE MATCHLESS REWARDS OF BOATING   8
by Carleton Mitchell

1   **THE UNIVERSE OF BOATS**   13

2   **HULL DESIGN: AN INTRICATE ART**   33

3   **HOW BOATS ARE BUILT**   71

4   **THE PUSH OR PULL TO MAKE IT GO**   93

5   **A PLACE FOR EVERYTHING**   115

6   **SHOPPING AROUND FOR A BOAT**   133

7   **WHERE TO BERTH A BOAT**   157

GLOSSARY   168

BIBLIOGRAPHY   171

CREDITS, ACKNOWLEDGMENTS   172

INDEX   173

The Matchless Rewards of Boating

The Matchless Rewards of Boating

By Carleton Mitchell

The boat is unique among the works of man. No other creation has existed so long with so little change. Minoan pottery and Egyptian tomb drawings depict craft similar to many still afloat in some parts of the world. But floating devices that may come under the Webster's dictionary definition of "a small vessel propelled by oars or paddles or by sail or power" existed much earlier. Primitive men ventured upon the water in vessels ranging from inflated animal skins to rafts of reed or wood. Thus the boat antedates the wheel, pottery and the domestication of animals and may even stand alongside the discovery of fire on the calendar of civilization.

In the Western world today, although many men still find their livelihood on the sea, by far the greatest number of boats are pleasure craft. And yet any boat, no matter how small, still means a way of life. Fundamentally, it provides escape, a magic carpet that puts the sailor completely on his own the moment he quits the shore. The important factors in his life become the state of the weather, the set of the sails, the rhythm of the engine, the distance and course to the next objective. Workaday worries seem to dissolve in the encircling water.

Equally appealing to the sailor is boating's endless challenge of expanding horizons. Start on an inland creek, and you find that the creek widens into a river, the river into a bay—which in turn opens onto the oceans of the world. In the same order, a person may begin with a dinghy, driven by either a little outboard or a wisp of sail. And then one day the dinghy is exchanged for a larger hull driven by more horsepower or a bigger rig—which may finally lead to an ocean-racing yawl Honolulu bound or a floating home anchored under pines or palms.

At every step, there is a carry-over of skills from the preceding stage. Yet a lifetime is not enough to absorb it all: learn to tie knots, and splices follow; master basic pilotage, and there comes the urge to know celestial navigation; acquire the rudiments of the mariner's precise vocabulary, and discover that its complexities and refinements are endless. But even for a beginner the pleasure and rewards are immediate.

Above all, boating is a sport. The response of a well-tuned sailing craft driven by a fresh breeze may be likened to soaring, to skiing, to surfing. There is the same surge and swoop, the same silent glide. In addition, with a fan of spray lifting forward and the wake stretching white astern, there comes the elation of being in harmony with the elements—and of harnessing them. A fast motorboat provides the same sense of elation, for different reasons: now it is not the silent glide, but the thrust of power. Water rushing past from a low viewpoint seems to move faster than the road moves past any shorebound vehicle, no matter what the actual speed may be.

But boats do not have to go fast to be satisfying. Some of my happiest moments have been aboard leisurely cruising boats. Bright in my memory across many years remains a passage from Havana to Nassau aboard *Carib,* my first big sailboat, a heavy 46-foot ketch. Even with the Gulf Stream current pushing us along for much of the way, our progress was slow but deeply satisfying. By day clouds piled above the blue rim of the horizon, by night stars reflected in long shimmering spears. Dawn and sunset colors were mirrored on a sea as smooth as an artist's palette. The silence was intense, the peace complete.

More recently, and in a different ocean, I encountered much the same conditions and sensations aboard a diesel-powered cruiser named *Sans Terre,* a 42-foot motorboat of fisherman lineage. We had left Newport Beach, California, bound south, and after a time the coast of Mexico began to unroll as a painted screen, while the Pacific lay as flat as the deserts inshore—no underlying swells, no ripples, nothing. As *Sans Terre* plowed along like a wind-up toy, majestic headlands loomed over the horizon and were swallowed

Author Carleton Mitchell relaxes at the wheel of his twin-diesel cruiser, Land's End. A mariner of surpassing skill, Mitchell has published seven books and scores of articles based on his lifetime of racing and cruising under both sail and power.

astern, until finally we left sight of land altogether to set our course for the remote Galápagos, 1,000 miles out on the Pacific. The murmur of the engines was soporific and I dozed and dreamed on my watches, and again during my turns below, thinking the thoughts that never seem to come into focus ashore. From these and similar memories evolved my cruising philosophy: When you are happy where you are, why be in a hurry to get somewhere else?

Although all of us who dream of boats are romantics, the approach to getting afloat must be practical. One of my own first nautical episodes was quite the opposite—a childhood misadventure in a rudderless skiff with a bed sheet for a sail. This taught me that some form of mechanical assistance, even oars, can be most useful in certain circumstances, as when a small boy is being carried to sea in an open boat by an unfriendly current. Since then I have resented the snobbishness of some windjammers in referring to motorboatmen as stinkpotters, because I recall being quite hungry, wet and scared—not necessarily in that order—before a good Samaritan came put-putting over the horizon to my rescue.

When a neophyte asks me what would be the right boat to buy as a starter, I am always in a quandary. A boat must be tailored to the individual, to his physical capabilities, to the amount of time and effort likely to be employed in mastering the fundamentals, to how and where the boat will be used. Other considerations are the skipper's age, the size of his midsection and of his pocketbook and, perhaps most important, the why implanted in his subconscious. If the prospective skipper can translate his vague dreams of being out on the water into more concrete concepts, there is less likelihood of his making a mistake in the original choice.

Undoubtedly the best approach for a beginner is to get a look at as many boats of as many different types as possible. For those living near areas where large fleets congregate—which includes most of the eastern and western seaboards of the United States, the Great Lakes, the Gulf Coast and many other areas—a good weekend sport is boat watching. Visit marinas, snoop around yacht clubs, sit with a pair of binoculars near a channel or point of land where there is a passing parade. Remember, you are not now trying to pick *the* boat, but are trying to find what type appeals. Try to imagine yourself in the cockpit or on the flying bridge, setting forth on that someday cruise. Do you feel strong stirrings when a husky motorboat designed like a trawler chuffs past, slow but sure? Or do you favor a faster cabin cruiser, with a bit of gleaming varnish and chrome? Do you admire a racing sloop with gung-ho crew leaping to wrestle down one jib and set another? Or do you see yourself cutting across your speedboat's curling wake on one ski, with the wind in your face and the spray flying?

Perhaps none of these options beckon, but there are others ad infinitum: power and sail, conservative and extreme, functional and flamboyant. Possibly it is the diversity of choice that has lured so many people to the water during the past few years. Hulls have been tailored for everyone, including the sedentary or the chronically seasick. For them, there is the flat-bottomed houseboat sitting placidly on a sheltered creek.

Potential boatmen who have no flotillas to watch can find other means of discovering the possibilities. Foremost is the printed page. In a boating publication the used-boat ads frequently contain the most interesting ideas—almost the equivalent of visiting a marina. Another means of getting acquainted with different hull forms, methods of propulsion and accessories is to visit a boat show, of which at least 100 are now scheduled annually in all parts of the country.

In making the fundamental choice between sail and power, it might well be wise to start with a craft driven wholly or at least principally by the wind. This is especially true for the younger and more active novices who wish to make boating a way of life. For a sailboat requires an immediate understanding of the elements and is more complex to manage. It is easier to make the transition from sail to power than the reverse. Yet, if from the start you are more drawn to the undeniable convenience and comfort of a motorboat, be not apologetic. The only right boat is the one that suits its owner and crew.

Regardless of type, the first boat should be the right size. The heartiest enthusiasm, to say nothing of friendships, may not survive a few miserable days in a too-small cockpit that is scorched by the sun or chilled by rain. But generally, too small is better than too big. The smaller the boat, the faster one's mistakes become apparent, and the easier it is to avoid serious consequences. A light outboard runabout approaching a dock too fast, for example, can be fended off by the skipper's foot, whereas a diesel cruiser might cause real damage to itself, the dock and the foot. Furthermore, the man who buys a boat that is too big and complicated to handle without skilled help not only misses many of the pleasures he expected to find afloat but is likely to remain a permanent novice.

Thus a beginner should select his first boat with the longer range viewpoint of becoming a competent boatman: from the moment a boat is sold, the man who wrote the check is transformed into a captain. Guests put their lives in his charge, literally, and other captains must depend upon him to know and observe procedures established for mutual safety. These include proper boat handling when docking and undocking, or picking up or dropping moorings; familiarity with buoyage systems and instant application of the rules of the road in crowded waters; the techniques of anchoring, maintaining a boat and checking on weather. In fact, I strongly believe that the man who thinks he wants a boat but who is unwilling to work at becoming a good seaman is better off ashore. Certainly his friends will be.

My own career began in 1922 on Lake Pontchartrain, near New Orleans, aboard a 20-foot sloop. Through the subsequent years I have known the thrills of many forms of competition afloat, from transatlantic and transpacific marathons under sail to riding the hottest of marine hot rods on the offshore powerboat circuit. For me, racing at any level is exciting. Undeniably, there is more apparent glamor to being part of a Bermuda Race fleet or an America's Cup defense than in making Sunday starts on Lake Winnebago. But there is little difference in tension and concentration after the preparatory gun sounds; from then on, it is not the size that matters, but the rewards to the individual. And those who do graduate to bigger boats will take along skills honed by the responsiveness of small hulls in close quarters.

One of the most satisfying of these skills is the skipper's capacity to sense his boat's special character—I might even say temperament. For instance, my 38-foot yawl, *Finisterre*, which I owned from 1954 to 1966, was built to go to sea and she knew it. Racing in light air and calm water on the Chesapeake or Long Island Sound or any other sheltered body, she would sulk. Competitors would simply sail away, and there was nothing that the crew could do about it. Yet let us be en route to Bermuda with similar conditions on the open ocean, and *Finisterre* would stubbornly stay with the fleet, waiting for the moment—her moment—when the wind piped up and the seas showed white teeth. Then we felt her come alive and could almost hear her croon: "Hang on, boys. Here we go!" And we did. Three times it happened, and three times in a row *Finisterre* was first in fleet. Cruising, she was as lazy as I was.

And cruising, I must confess, has now become my own special love. To go places in one's own boat has a dreamlike quality. Like a contented turtle, the cruising man carries his house wherever he goes. I can remember stealing through the rocky Baltic reefs of Sweden and Finland, under the midnight sun, where the somber forests sigh like the music of Sibelius. Equally sharp are memories of swinging at anchor to the warm trade winds, a palm-girt beach over the bow gleaming in moonlight. I have been at home, in the fullest sense of the word, surrounded by pictures of personal meaning, books that were old friends and other mementos linking me to the past.

Perhaps the most extraordinary aspect of cruising is the manner in which short passages can open whole new perspectives. You may have lived on the shore of a lake, bay or river for years and think you know it well. But then go

Mitchell's onetime favorite, the 38-foot, yawl Finisterre, rises gracefully to an Atlantic swell. In 1956, 1958 and 1960 she carried the author to overall victory in the Newport-Bermuda ocean race.

A home at sea, Mitchell's 62-foot Land's End reflects his change in preference from sail to power. Built in Hong Kong, the vessel has lines that blend seaworthiness with world-ranging cruising comfort.

in your boat to the other side, and a new world seems to open. Along with this fresh perspective come live challenges—where do I anchor, how much scope should I use, what if the wind shifts during the night? And these challenges must be met quickly. For wherever your interests lead you, there are fundamentals that apply to all boats and boatmen.

Foremost is the concept of safety. The sailor must never forget that no matter how alluring the water or how much at home he may feel on its surface, it is an alien element. The more experienced a seaman becomes, the more careful he is, for he understands the power of the sea and knows how fast its moods can change. He knows, too, that danger lurks not only on the open ocean.

I learned this lesson on Chesapeake Bay aboard Finisterre's predecessor, a 58-foot yawl named Caribbee, after returning from the Transatlantic Race of 1952. One Sunday morning we were ghosting along on the mirror-flat bay, sliding lazily past fishermen in anchored skiffs. Later, a haze began to gather over the western shore, developed into a smudge, then became a black cloud; but the sun still shone and the breeze remained light. Caribbee had just rounded into Eastern Bay, a wide tributary of the Chesapeake, with more fishing skiffs around, when all hell broke loose. The squall's first blast ripped our jib to shreds, while the pressure of wind on the mainsail laid our sturdy ocean racer almost flat on her side. Within seconds wavelets were running across the face of the bay; these became waves, and then cresting seas breaking aboard. We were transformed from a relaxed group into a panic party.

In 3,000 miles of North Atlantic Ocean we had encountered nothing so fierce. Caribbee came through unscathed, except for the jib, but the fishermen in their little boats were not so lucky. Several were lost. It happens every year, even on sheltered inland lakes. That day on the Chesapeake, nature had sent up signals, but for different reasons we had all ignored them. Eternal vigilance is the price of safety.

Possibly the best advice I can pass along to a budding boatman is this: Never fail to follow the dictates of your own judgment. No matter what others may say, if you don't like the look of the sky, shorten sail when you think you should. Run back to shelter if the engine doesn't sound right. Don't stay overnight in an exposed anchorage if the wind doesn't smell right. You may turn out to have been overcautious, but better that than deep trouble.

Almost every bad moment I have experienced afloat came after a warning bell had sounded in the back of my mind, to be rationalized away. Even that day on the Chesapeake I was guilty. "A squall is brewing," I told myself a dozen times during the afternoon, yet each time added, "but it probably won't hit until we're anchored." Undoubtedly the drowned fishermen had argued against their better judgment with a variation on the same theme, especially if the fish were biting.

In the final analysis, the rewards of boating are mostly personal. There is pride in a well-turned splice, satisfaction in safely threading a tricky channel, elation in driving through an opening on the starting line. No galleries rise to cheer the man working on a slippery pitch-dark foredeck or to applaud the successful running of a rough inlet, for boating is not a spectator sport. The sailor's desire to cross oceans in small craft must be likened to the urge that drives other men to climb distant, difficult mountains. And yet one does not have to cross oceans to savor the inner rewards of achievement.

Thus the boat can mean to the individual all I have promised and more. Boating is the glint of summer sun on wavelets or watching autumn leaves drift past the cockpit; it is a wriggling fish coming aboard, and the steaming pot announcing chowder for dinner; it is lying in a warm bunk listening to the whine of wind in the rigging. It is sunshine on a bare back, moonlight in a long, shimmering path, clouds towering into the sky. It is the purr of a motor or the creak of lines through blocks and the splash of the anchor in a new harbor. It is the exhilaration of a brisk beat to windward, spray like flung jewels and salt on the lips—or it is simply resting quietly, looking out at the sky and the water, full of peace.

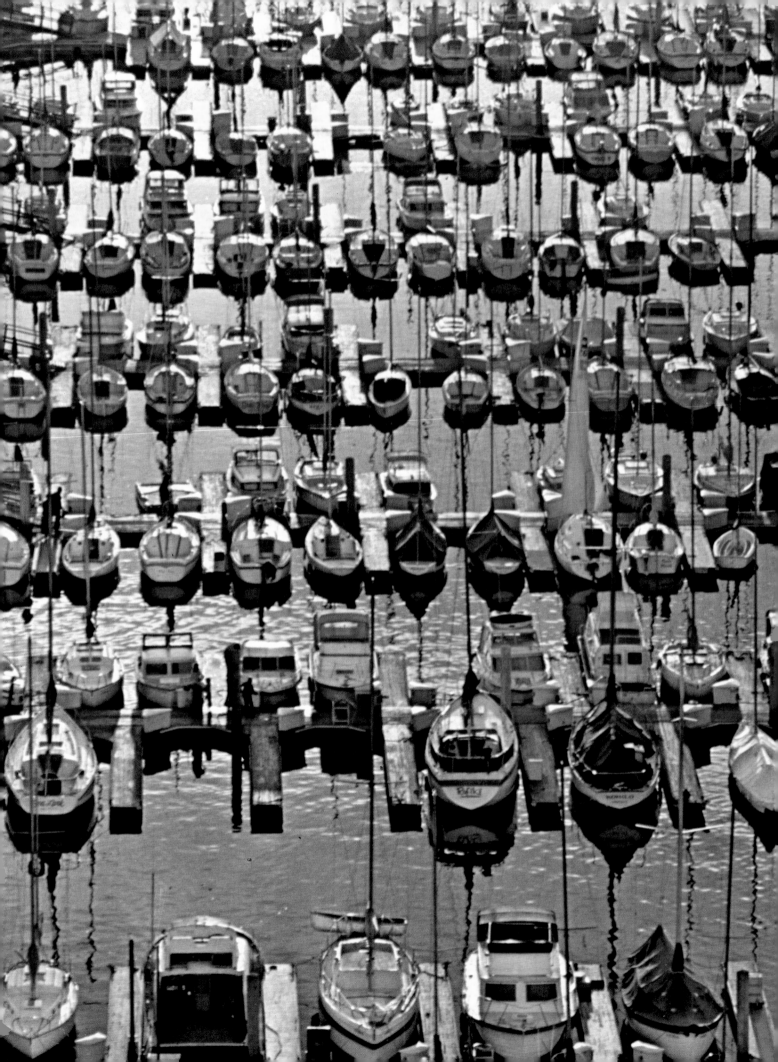

1 From the sandy inlets of Chesapeake Bay to the fir-trimmed reaches of Puget Sound, no people on earth dispose of so much navigable water as Americans. Nor does anyone else have a choice of pleasure craft in such a rich, bewildering range of classes and prices, shapes and sizes: inboards and outboards and even surfboards sporting scraps of sail; floating patios called houseboats; racing yachts of prodigious cost and complexity; swift runabouts and slowpoke rowboats that can carry anyone with a picnic hamper into a midsummer day's dream.

There are more than 10 million pleasure boats in America. Almost 50 million water-struck folk annually spend over four billion dollars to enjoy them.

THE UNIVERSE OF BOATS

The geographical range of their enjoyment is spectacularly varied—and far from limited to natural waters. In 1936 the Hoover Dam was completed and backed up Lake Mead to give Nevada and Arizona 229 square miles of watery playground. Since then, the boatman's realm has been extended by thousands of square miles of man-made lakes. Ever-increasing streams of boats and boat trailers flow where not long before there was only dust or desert. On the Texas-Oklahoma border, where the Red River has been stalled to form sprawling Texoma Lake, as many as 4,000 boats churn the waters on a single day.

A sailor in the United States can choose among at least 250 different varieties of small sailboat classes; some of them, like the ubiquitous Sunfish—numbering tens of thousands of boats—summon racing skippers to regattas all over the country and even the world. Ocean racing, once a game for a rich and happy handful, now calls up hundreds of sails at a time to starting lines in New England, Florida and California. Those who want to do their ocean racing inland can take on the challenging waters of the Great Lakes.

These are only a few signs of an extraordinary revolution that has occurred in the last two decades to make boating a mass sport. The growth has been spurred in part by the perfection of durable synthetic materials—notably fiberglass for mass production of hulls and substances like nylon and Dacron for stronger, virtually rotproof ropes and sails. But as much as anything, the revolution was stimulated by the triumph of the outboard motor: though introduced to a skeptical public in the late 19th Century, more than 50 years passed before that cranky monster matured into the dependable engine that now speeds some eight million outboard owners around their favorite waters.

In some ways, what has happened with boats resembles the earlier metamorphosis of cars—when the mass-producing of automobiles made it possible for the men who made them to buy them. The Marina del Rey in Los Angeles, California *(left)*, is, in fact, a seagoing parking lot. But there is an essential difference between boats and cars. More than any land-bound vehicle, boats offer freedom. They need not follow prescribed grids of concrete or asphalt but can cruise wherever whim and depth of water may dictate. Each shining deck at left represents a dream of escape or speed, of peace or elemental challenge.

The difficulty of learning the skills needed to achieve a similar dream may deter some who fear being labeled landlubbers. But such timidity is needless today: there are dozens of books and hundreds of courses offered by boat clubs and associations that teach everything from boat handling to nautical cookery *(page 171)*. Besides, boatmen are a friendly breed; a neophyte will not have to look far to find counsel—usually no farther than the other side of the dock. Actually, the hardest problem facing a newcomer may well be choosing his first boat from among the array of options open to him. Here, too, advice from experienced boatmen will help—and the galaxy of boats on the following pages is offered as another aid in sorting out the options.

Burnished by late sunlight, a peaceful armada at California's vast Marina del Rey attests to the boundless array of pleasure craft.

Basic Boats

The 20-foot canoe at left, made of aluminum with a stern squared to take a motor, is an exotic relative of the familiar double-ended canoe that millions of Americans have paddled on fishing jaunts, camping trips and Sunday outings on virtually every lake and pond in the land.

The humble rowboat, typified by the 10-footer lazily drifting below, is perhaps the most uncomplicated of all pleasure craft. Whether used as a tender to a larger boat or on its own, the rowboat is the vessel in which many a seaman has learned the fundamentals of boat handling.

Originally developed by Eskimos to weather open Arctic water, the kayak (above) has been adopted by white-water enthusiasts across the nation. The boat's fiberglass construction, tiny cockpit and watertight decking make it especially seaworthy, and the low position of the paddler, who sits on the bottom, adds to the stability of the craft.

Easy-to-Handle Sailboats

These fleet little sloops of the Flying Junior class, running downwind on Lake Tahoe in the High Sierra, are among the hundreds of kinds of small racing sailboats that dot the lakes, rivers and protected coastal waters of the U.S.—and much of the rest of the world. The Juniors are made of fiberglass, measure 13 feet 6 inches and weigh 250 pounds. Like others of their type, they are lively to sail, but relatively stable and forgiving of novices' mistakes. They are convenient, too: they can be speedily unrigged and easily transported overland on a trailer.

The so-called board boat, epitomized by these Sunfish racing on Rhode Island's Barrington River, is probably the simplest form of modern sailboat—and it is certainly the most popular one. An elaboration of the surfboard, equipped with mast, sail and rudder, these unpretentious craft have no proper cockpit, but usually contain a small footwell. Though many types of board boats are keenly raced, like the ones shown here, their principal appeal is that they are rugged, portable and, above all, easy to sail. They are, in sum, the perfect craft for beginners.

High-Performance Craft

Twin-hulled derivatives of the South Seas outrigger canoe, modern-day catamarans, such as this 20-footer with one hull in the air, provide exciting sailing for growing numbers of enthusiasts. Catamarans have different performance characteristics from single-hulled boats, so that sailors of conventional craft have to learn new skills in cats—such as the trick of sailing with one hull out of the water. Although some cats are large enough for ocean cruising, most are day sailers in the 14- to 20-foot range. Catamarans have reached their greatest popularity in California where a number of the hottest designs have evolved.

The Tempest-class sloop, like this one cutting close to a course marker on Long Island Sound, is a sophisticated racing machine that keeps an experienced crew busy—and wet. While the skipper sits out, or hikes, as far as possible to keep the boat upright, his crewman gets even farther out by hanging in a wire sling appropriately known as a trapeze. Measuring 22 feet overall, the Tempest is more elaborate—and somewhat more expensive—than many other high-performance boats.

The low-slung, blunt-bowed craft skittering swiftly across New Jersey's Barnegat Bay (right) are E-class scows, 28 feet of sensitive, exacting racing boat. The "E" is one of many classes of scows raced by sailors on sheltered waters. Flat-bottomed and requiring better than average seamanship and agility to sail properly, the scows were developed in Canada and the Midwest around the turn of the century, proliferated in the Great Lakes region and eventually spread south and east.

Powerboats for Fishing

Sturdy, roomy, business-like, a utility craft such as this open 19-footer provides a stable fishing platform and has the speed to get quickly to the choice angling grounds. A boat of this type can carry two outboards of up to 75 horsepower each. These engines will push the boat to over 30 mph—but will eat up a lot of gas in the process. The central control station (with an offset steering wheel in this instance) is a practical arrangement that provides extra work space. Without the two outboard motors, the boat costs about as much as an average family sedan; fitted with the largest engines, the price is nearly twice as much.

Designed to ride comfortably in rough waters, boats like this sporty 24-foot fishing craft are usually found on the ocean or large bays. With a V-bottomed hull that cleaves the waves, and two inboard-outboard motors—hybrids in which outboard-style steering propellers connect to inboard engines—the boat can travel at speeds of more than 40 mph. It has a small cabin equipped with basic accommodations for two: a pair of bunks, a head and a small galley with an alcohol stove.

Boats for Special Tastes

A lovely restored antique boat like the one at right arouses in old-boat enthusiasts the same passion that an elderly automobile does in collectors of antique cars. This gleaming pleasure launch, built circa 1907, is a survivor of the gilded pre-World War I era when squadrons of similar elegant toys ferried vacationing American millionaires around Ontario's Lake Muskoka. It knifes along at a smart 30 mph, but what appeals to the antiques collector is not the craft's speed but that 32-foot expanse of hand-rubbed mahogany and burnished brass.

Two contented mariners, each with eyes only for the course dead ahead, pass close at hand, piloting 7-foot plastic water scooters. Mini-craft such as these, intended purely for pleasure, are made in any number of whimsical designs—disks, dragons, swans, fish—and are propelled by pedal power, electric motor or, as in these two, by small inboard engines.

Offshore Cruisers and Fishermen

All the comforts of a sumptuous home are available in the 70-foot cabin cruiser at left, which represents the ultimate in stock boats, i.e., those that are not individually designed for custom buyers. Made of fiberglass and powered by twin diesels, this craft luxuriously accommodates eight passengers in staterooms with shower-equipped baths, plus a crew of two. Such a floating castle can cost well over $400,000 if it is equipped with such amenities as air conditioning, soundproofing, washer-dryer, freezer, stereo and sophisticated electronic navigation equipment.

This 36-foot fiberglass sports cruiser is ideal for offshore sport fishing. Its outside steering controls are mounted on a high platform, called a flying bridge, to provide the skipper all-around visibility; two powerful inboard engines whisk the boat from one fishing spot to the next at up to 35 mph, and its large cockpit gives the angler ample working space. The boat sleeps four or more, and has toilet and shower and full cooking arrangements.

Cabin cruisers such as this inboard-powered 26-footer are used for fishing and cruising on every large body of water in the United States. Many boats of similar but smaller design, usually able to accommodate four people comfortably, are also built for outboard power.

Custom Cruisers

This sturdy, custom-built 69-footer is a splendid example of a powerboat especially designed to get its passengers somewhere comfortably and get them there fast. Though boasting a speedy underbody and powerful engines, it eschews flashy streamlining in favor of a traditional-looking superstructure.

Sailboats for Cruising or Racing

The 75-foot yawl Blackfin (right), driving at high speed through Atlantic swells, was designed primarily to lead her competitors to the finish line of long-distance ocean races. Yachts like this are custom-built at great expense to the maximum length allowed by international racing rules and are planned in every detail for fast sailing, though they are also equipped for comfortable—if hardly economical—long-range cruising.

With their colorful spinnakers flying, these moderate-sized sloops shown racing in New England waters are just as well suited for family cruising. Measuring about 35 feet, they can be easily handled by a small crew —as few as two persons—although they sleep up to six in some comfort. Equipped with an auxiliary engine, stove, icebox and toilet, they can be self-sufficient for up to a month, either at sea or on sizable waters.

Floating Houses

Armchair comfort, bright sunlight on a still backwater and a made-to-order diving platform —these are a few quiet joys offered by the homey houseboat. Like this one moored at the edge of the Tennessee River, houseboats are at their best in tranquil waters because their boxy shape—which encloses most of the conveniences to be found in a land-bound home—makes them uncomfortable in rough conditions. Houseboats come in all sizes from 20 to 60 feet, and though some do more than 30 mph, many poke along powered by nothing more than a 10-horsepower outboard.

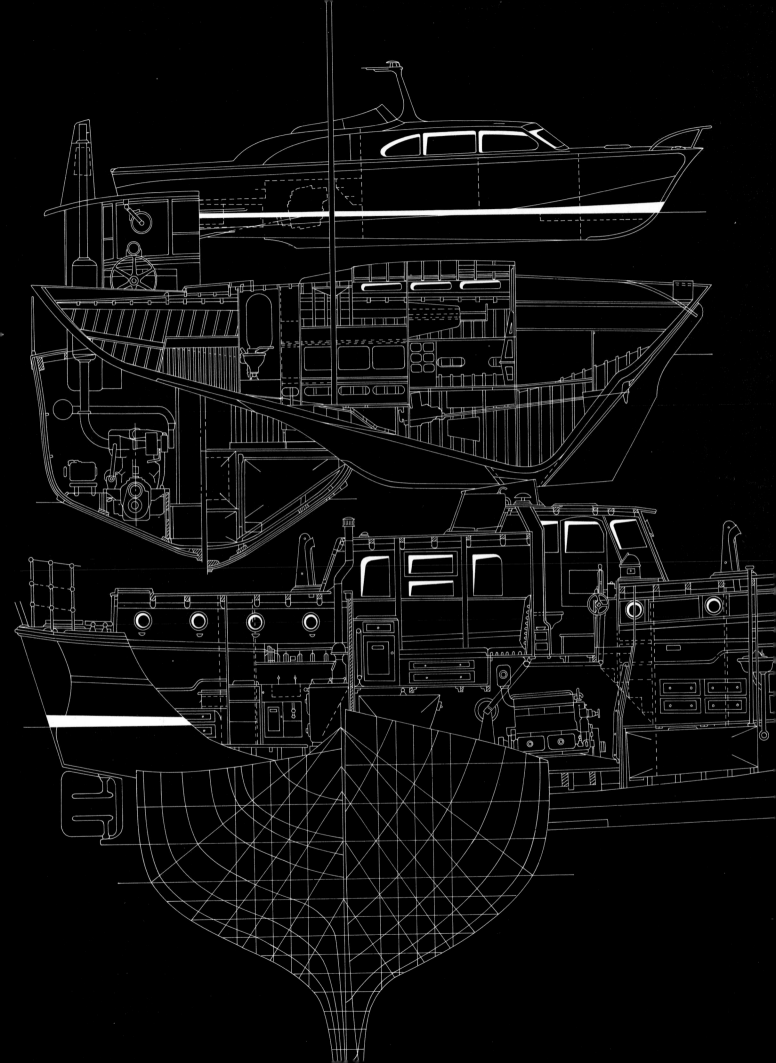

2 Few of man's creations are designed to do as many things—most of them contradictory—as is the hull of a boat. Clearly, the hull must float, even if constructed of materials that themselves do not float. It must be wide and stable enough to stay upright in tossing seas and yet sufficiently streamlined to move smoothly through them. It must be at once comparatively light yet tremendously strong: a cubic yard of water weighs just under a ton, and although a hull rides over most waves, the few that catch it wrong carry a good many cubic yards apiece.

Besides these universal demands, there are the functional imperatives im-

HULL DESIGN: AN INTRICATE ART

posed by the divergent needs and tastes of boatowners. Many hulls must contain kitchens, bunks, toilets, closets, drawers, tables—despite the fact that most of these tend to be squarish while boats are typically curved. Some hulls are made to go fast, some to be extra sturdy, some to be beautiful, some to be inexpensive. Some, impossibly, are asked to be all of these things.

The truth is that no hull shape does everything well. In sail as well as power, roomy cruisers are likely to be slow, sleek racers are often crowded and uncomfortable. The most easily driven hull at one speed turns out to be less satisfactory at another speed.

In general, sailboats pose more problems than do powerboats. With a motorboat the amount of power is controlled by the skipper; thrust always comes from behind, and the boat normally operates in an upright position. A sailboat, on the other hand, is moved by the errant force of wind against its sails. This pressure on its sails tends to make the boat lean over—or heel—and to thrust it sideways as much as push it forward. These tendencies must be counteracted. Moreover, a sailboat is expected to perform well whether it is upright or heeled over.

Given this bundle of problems, the development of naval architecture has been a slow one. In the past, ships served well if they simply carried their cargoes from port to port in coastal waters, and the need for speed or crew comfort was considered secondary. Columbus made his voyages in clumsy trading vessels that were never meant to cross oceans. Over a century later the Pilgrims gave thanks for crossing the Atlantic at an average speed of two miles per hour. Gradually, mercantile interests forced the design of faster ships: privateers that eluded blockading warships, clippers that raced for the richest markets, fishermen that could get to the Grand Banks and back in a hurry.

The pressure of the 20th Century boating boom speeded the evolutionary pace with its demand for faster and more efficient craft. In response, designers have developed new species of high-performance boats, using exotic shapes, modern building materials and streamlined construction methods to achieve optimums of effectiveness and of compromise with the varying demands put upon a vessel. Today's houseboat may go to sea; large seagoing sailboats are designed along lines previously confined to surface-skimming Sunday afternoon racing craft. Nevertheless, there are still certain fundamental hull types that do certain things best, and these types, their components, shapes and functions are examined in the following pages.

The evolution of hull design continues, but it is still far from being a precise science. The greatest yacht designer of the last century, Nathanael Herreshoff, created hull shapes by carving models of them; today computers and elaborate testing tanks are the naval architect's tools. And yet designers are still remarkably unsuccessful at predicting exactly how a boat will behave at sea; some of Captain Nat's skills have never been surpassed. Inspiration and more than a touch of art are still basic ingredients in every good hull.

A montage of naval architects' drawings reveals the precise details of a hull's structure, which must accommodate all the demands imposed by function and the owner's taste.

Definitions and Dimensions

The hull is a boat's essential element, and everything else—masts, sails, engines, superstructure—develops from it. Each sector or curve or measurement of a hull has a precise and specific name, and though most of the names are relics of an earlier age, their meanings still apply. A few terms refer to directions on the hull, e.g., forward is toward the front, aft is toward the rear and amidships is in between. Something located behind something else is abaft of it, and anywhere behind the hull itself is astern. Two other terms are general nautical directional words: to a person looking forward, the right side is the starboard side, the left is port.

The hulls of sailboats have been used in the illustrations at near right simply because their shapes are more complex below the waterline than those of powerboats. But the definitions associated with them are shared by virtually all hulls.

One of the most significant measurements of a hull is the weight, generally expressed in terms of displacement *(top far right)*. The total displacement is dictated by the law of gravity: Any object placed on the water's surface will sink just far enough to move aside—or displace—a weight of water equal to that of the object. If the object is dense, like a steel ball, for example, it will sink. A boat's steel hull will float, however, since the metal is not concentrated in a lump, but encloses a volume of air that, even combined with the weight of the steel, weighs less than an equal volume of water.

At rest all hulls displace their weight in water. But when in motion they divide into two major categories. One type continues to push aside its weight of water as it moves; this is a displacement hull. The other type, called a planing hull, is designed to rise partly out of the water at high speeds and skim the waves on a flattish bottom. In either type, the amount of water the hull must push aside remains a key factor in its design.

The arrows in this diagram indicate a hull's four basic measurements. Length of the waterline, or LWL, is measured at the water level. The distance from this to the bottom of the keel is the boat's draft and equals the least depth of water the boat can operate in, i.e., the amount it draws. Beam is the maximum breadth. Length overall, or LOA, is the boat's greatest length, not counting protrusions like bowsprits or rudders.

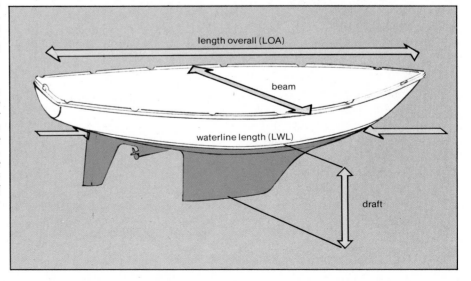

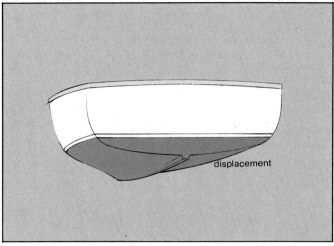

A hull settles into the water until it displaces an amount of water (dark blue) that weighs the same as the boat. The hull floats instead of sinking because, taken as a whole, it is less dense than water; thus the small volume of water displaced by the hull's submerged portion weighs as much as the whole hull.

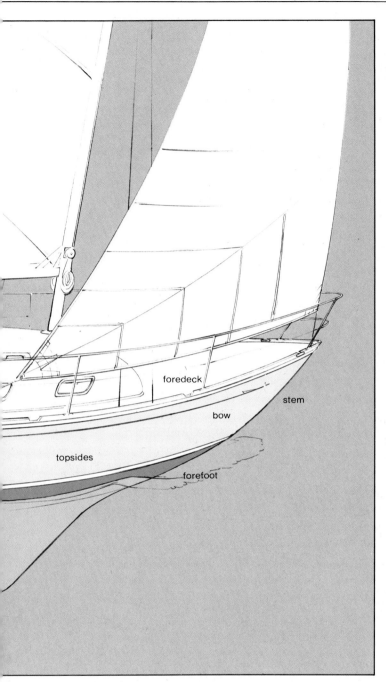

Some of the hull's parts, such as bow, stern, deck, keel, are familiar enough even to landlubbers, but others may need defining. The topsides are the boat's sides between the waterline and the rail. The stem is the forwardmost part of the bow, and the area where it joins the keel below the waterline is called the forefoot. Run describes the underwater part of the stern, while the counter rises from the waterline and ends in a transom. The cockpit, fenced in by the coaming, is a well from which the boat is steered, with a tiller, as here, or a wheel. The companionway leads to the cabin below.

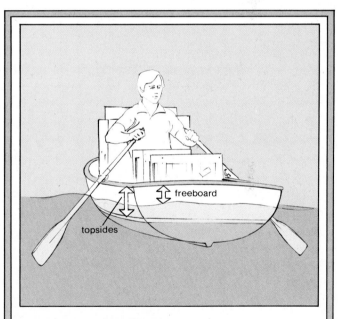

Topsides and Freeboard

A boat's topsides are the sides of the hull between the theoretical waterline and the rail. (Topsides is not to be confused with topside, which is where a sailor goes when he climbs up on deck from down below.) The topsides measurement is constant whether the boat is in the water or not. Freeboard measures the distance from the actual water level to the rail, and it varies as the water level does. If freeboard is reduced too much, the boat is in danger of being swamped by water coming in over the rail—as anyone in a boat overloaded like the one above is apt to learn.

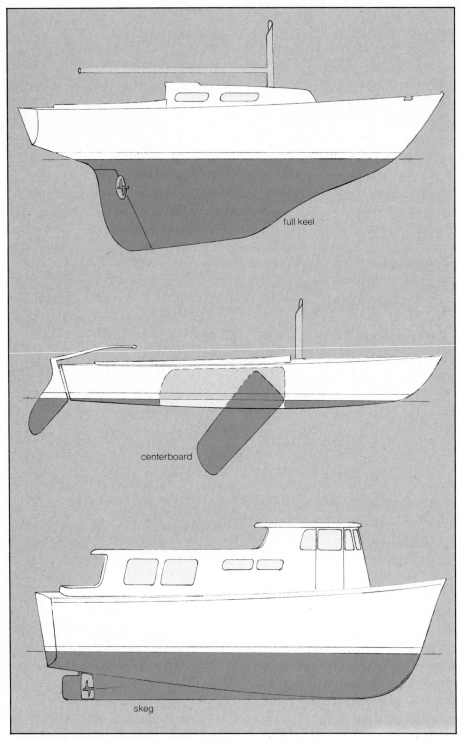

full keel

centerboard

skeg

A displacement sailboat generally has a deep keel that is often ballasted, or weighted, to provide stability. In many sailboats, particularly in small ones, the retractable centerboard is relatively light; it resists sideslip but adds little to the craft's stability. The bottom of a heavy, displacement-type powerboat normally has a straight, shallow keel with a sloping extension, called a skeg, that helps keep the boat moving in a straight line and protects the propeller and rudder from underwater obstructions.

Contours and Profiles

Every type of hull has a characteristic look, a recognizable blending of subtle curves and contours. Some of the hull's distinctive lines are functional, others are esthetic, and the seaman's eye learns to judge from them a boat's performance as well as its beauty.

Below the waterline a hull's configuration is strictly functional. Here the most conspicuous feature is likely to be the keel *(top left)*—or the lack of it. Technically a keel is the longitudinal member that acts as the hull's structural backbone. In ordinary usage, though, the word applies to the vertical addition that extends downward from a hull's bottom.

Most sailboats have such keels because they need some vertical underwater surface to keep them from sliding sideways under pressure from the wind. In most large- and medium-sized sailboats this lateral resistance is provided primarily by a fixed keel. Smaller sailboats commonly use a retractable variation of the keel, called a centerboard, which can be raised and lowered. Generally boats whose bottom profiles are interrupted only by a centerboard are likely to be more lively—and perhaps less seaworthy—than their deep-keeled cousins.

Motorboats, not subject to the sideways push of wind in sails, tend not to have much in the way of keels; and even heavy, seagoing powerboats *(left)* have relatively simple bottom profiles.

Another underwater clue to a boat's performance is found in a measurement called deadrise. Most clearly seen from bow on, deadrise is the angle at which the bottom slants upward from the keel. The smaller the angle of deadrise, the flatter a boat's bottom is and the more easily it skims over calm waters—but the more percussively, also, it pounds against the waves of a rough sea.

There is one other major underwater contour that shows up best from a head-on view. It is known as the turn of the bilge, i.e., the contour where the bottom meets the topsides (the bilge is the area inside the hull next to the bottom). Here, too, function often dictates form. A sharply angled turn of the bilge, also called a hard chine, works effectively with the straight sides and flat bottom of a shallow-draft, planing powerboat.

From the waterline up, though, esthetic considerations take on more importance, as in the curvature of the topsides *(top far right)*. An analysis of the hull's other major above-water features follows on pages 38 and 39.

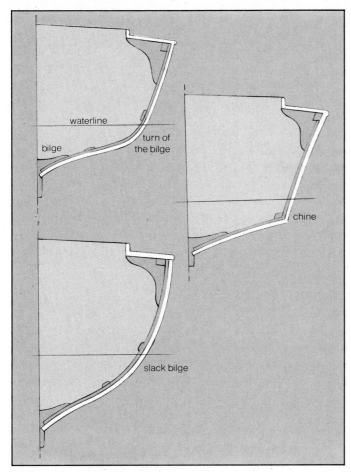

waterline

bilge

turn of
the bilge

chine

slack bilge

The intersection of bottom and topsides may
be a conventionally rounded turn of
the bilge, a hard angle, called a chine, or a
gently curved slack bilge. Chine is common
to the flattish undersides of small, high-speed
powerboats, while the slack bilge is often
found in seagoing, deep-keeled craft.

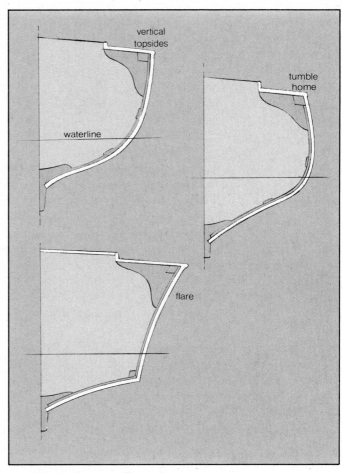

vertical
topsides

tumble
home

waterline

flare

The topsides of many hulls rise almost
vertically, some curve back in with a contour
called tumble home, while others flare
outward. Most sailboats' sides are relatively
straight, but many powerboats have flared
bows that help deflect spray, and tumble
home farther aft, designed chiefly for looks.

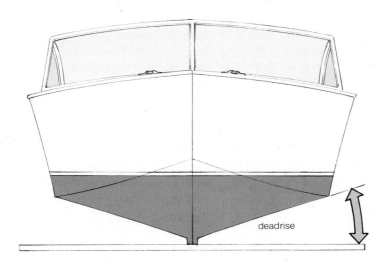

deadrise

The angle at which a boat's bottom rises
from horizontal on either side of the
centerline is deadrise, drawn here at about
18°. An angle less than 20° produces a
flattish bottom suited for speed in sheltered
waters; an angle more than 20°, called steep
deadrise, is typical of boats designed
for heavy sea conditions. In some hulls, to
combine speed with seaworthiness, the
deadrise varies from bow to stern (page 43).

Bows

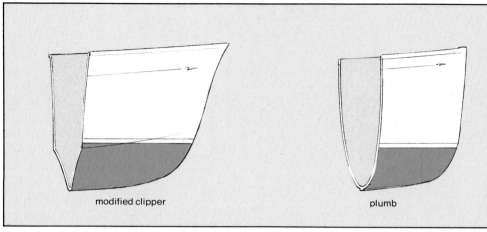

modified clipper   plumb

A sampling of pleasure-boat bow shapes reflects function as well as the traditions of form. The modified clipper bow, reminiscent of the arcing stems of great sailing ships, is often seen on powerboats, where its handsome flare serves as a spray deflector. The plumb bow, used on both power and sailing craft, is a traditional shape, taken from workboats and sailing catboats of the late 19th Century.

Sterns

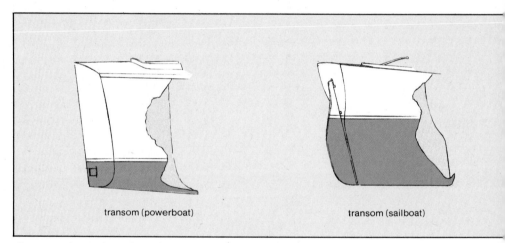

transom (powerboat)   transom (sailboat)

The sterns of many boats feature a vertical transom that descends directly from the deck to the waterline. This design, especially common to large power craft, allows a full, deep cockpit to run all the way aft. The sailboat's transom stern, with the rudder mounted on it instead of being attached to the hull underwater, is an easily constructed shape dating back to oldtime workboats.

Sheer

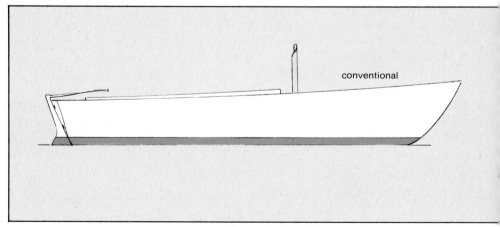

conventional

Sheer is the top line of a hull's profile. And of all the boat's contours it is perhaps the one most dependent on esthetic convention. The traditional sheer consists of a graceful curve that is higher at bow and stern than amidships. The line harks back to sailing vessels of the past whose forward and after sections were prominently raised. Until a few decades ago most boats had this conventional sheer line.

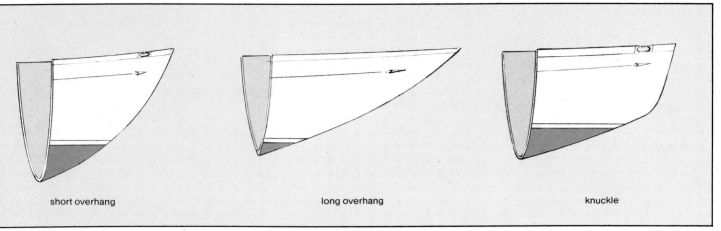

| short overhang | long overhang | knuckle |

These three sailboat bows are all raked, unlike the plumb bow, and belong to hulls whose overall length is substantially greater than their waterline length. The short overhang is common to modern, light-displacement craft, while the long overhang is more usual on heavier cruiser-racers. The knuckle is essentially a variation on the long overhanging bow—with the tip cut off to save weight.

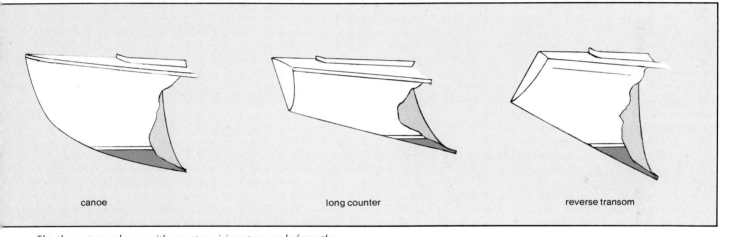

| canoe | long counter | reverse transom |

The three sterns above, with counters rising at an angle from the waterline, are normally found on sailboats, although some elderly power yachts sport canoe sterns. On a sailboat the canoe stern lends a double-ended look especially popular in Europe. The long counter with a small transom usually appears on a boat with a long overhanging bow; the reverse transom serves mainly to save weight.

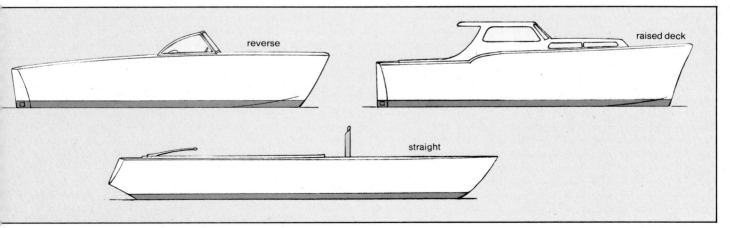

Modern styles in sheer lines have departed radically from the conventional curve. Straight sheer has become common on sailboats, partly because modern design in larger yachts tends toward boats with higher topsides to provide more generous accommodations below. Reverse sheer, though seen on a few sailboats, is more typical of speedboats, while the raised deck is familiar on cabin cruisers.

Resistance and Drag

Water is an incompressible substance that strongly resists a boat's efforts to plow through it. Designing a hull that will best overcome this resistance is one of the naval architect's most vexing problems.

Among the many factors the designer must cope with is the frictional drag between the water and the hull's submerged, or wetted, surface. The more wetted surface a hull has, the more power is needed to drive it along. But the parts that increase the hull's wetted surface, such as a keel or a rudder, are necessary to steady the boat in the water, providing steering control and preventing sideslip.

Thus the designer's dilemma includes the need to keep wetted surface to a minimum while ensuring a hull shape that will remain stable and under control. The solution, as in so much of yacht design, lies in realistic compromise.

A less critical but still a measurable factor of frictional resistance is the turbulence caused by any protuberances or roughness on the hull's underwater surface, such as pipe outlets. Even if such protuberances are small, each one takes its toll in speed.

Finally, no normal displacement hull can escape the tyranny of the ultimate source of aquatic resistance: wave making. The water displaced by a hull in motion piles up into a wave system that moves with the hull, increasing in size as the hull picks up speed until there is a wave crest at the bow and at the stern, with a trough in between. At this point the displacement hull becomes captive of its own wave system. For it is a physical property of water that a wave of a certain size travels at a certain speed—the longer the wave, the faster the speed and vice versa. Thus a boat, generating its own wave, ultimately is trapped between crests. The wave can be no longer than the boat's waterline length, and the boat can travel only as fast as a wave of that length can move. This velocity is called hull speed.

The only way to exceed this naturally imposed speed limit is to make hulls light enough and sufficiently flat-bottomed so that instead of pushing through the water they plane on top of it. When a planing hull breaks the bondage of wave resistance this way *(opposite, bottom)*, its top speed is determined less by its waterline length than by the amount of power—whether from engine or wind—that pushes it. Planing so effectively beats water resistance that it is key to the design of most modern powerboats *(pages 42-46)* and a growing number of sailboats *(page 52)*.

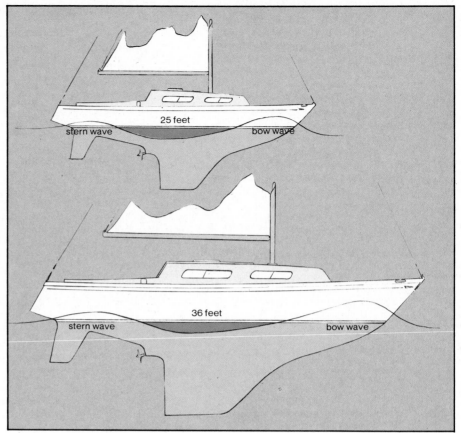

These two craft illustrate the hydrodynamic principle that limits a displacement boat's top speed. The smaller one, which has a 25-foot waterline, is theoretically confined to the speed a 25-foot wave moves, about 7 mph; the other, at 36 feet, can move up to 9 mph.

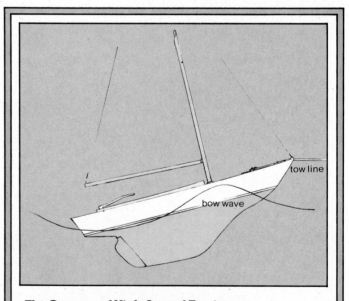

The Danger of High-Speed Towing

If a displacement hull is towed by another boat at a velocity much beyond its hull speed, the results can be disastrous. The hull, in moving faster, produces a longer wave, so that the stern crest moves back; the stern drops into the trough and the hull is forced to breast the water in an awkward, tilted-up position. Under such unnatural strain the hull might suffer structural damage; at the least it will slew around wildly, and at worst it might swamp.

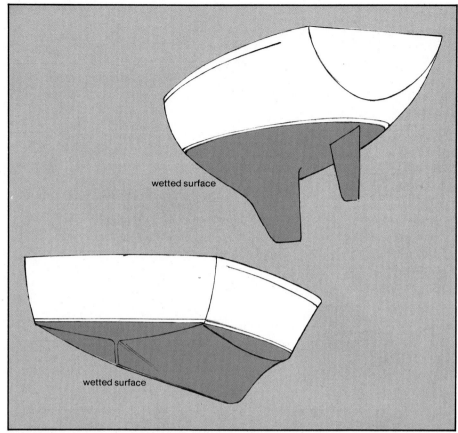

wetted surface

wetted surface

Any protuberances on a vessel's underbody, such as the rounded end of a water intake pipe (shown below with its valve, or seacock), add to frictional drag by causing turbulence in the flow of water along the hull. Like a rock in a stream, the projection deflects the water in eddies that fan out behind it; this area of disturbance inhibits the boat's speed.

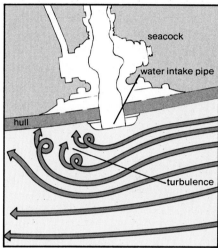

seacock

water intake pipe

hull

turbulence

Variations in the amount of friction-producing wetted surface of different hulls are demonstrated above by a relatively flat-bottomed skiff (left) and a sailboat with keel and rudder. The skiff's shape offers little surface area—or resistance—but has nothing to prevent sideways slippage. The sailboat's keel resists slipping and its rudder gives firm steering control, but both add wetted surface and hence drag.

Skimming the surface, a planing hull at high speed lifts most of its bulk out of the water, thereby escaping the wave-making resistance that limits the speed of a displacement hull. Thus elevated, the hull also presents a minimum of wetted surface, which further reduces the water's drag. However, a lot of power is needed to shove the hull up onto a plane; the heavier the load, the more power is required.

The Simple Flat Bottom

The simplest hull shape is little more than a straight-sided, flat-bottomed box with perhaps some curvature at bow and stern. Such a shape, besides being easy to build, is extremely stable since its wide bottom resists tipping. It is also easy to propel through the water because it has less wetted surface than a hull with complex contours below the waterline; and it draws less water than a hull that has a rounded bottom or a keel.

These advantages are particularly suited to the design of the houseboat, which must provide a stable, roomy platform for a large number of passengers and which need venture no farther than the calm, shallow margins of rivers and lakes.

Yet the flat bottom has two drawbacks that seriously impair its usefulness. First, although it is easily driven, its shape provides no lateral resistance when underway, so that the vessel is likely to slide sideways in turns, making it hard to maneuver. The design's other chief drawback is that in rough water it provides a jarring ride. As power is applied to the stern of a hull the bow rises; the flat bottom moving rapidly in such an attitude meets each successive wave with a blow that is like the slap of an open hand, an unpleasant characteristic known as pounding.

Because of these defects, the truly flat-bottomed hull has become rare in modern design, especially since the use of fiberglass has simplified the problem of molding enough contour into a hull to ensure improved control and a smoother ride. Some houseboats of old-fashioned design as well as many skiffs and barges still feature uncompromisingly flat bottoms, but nowadays the most advanced houseboats come with curves.

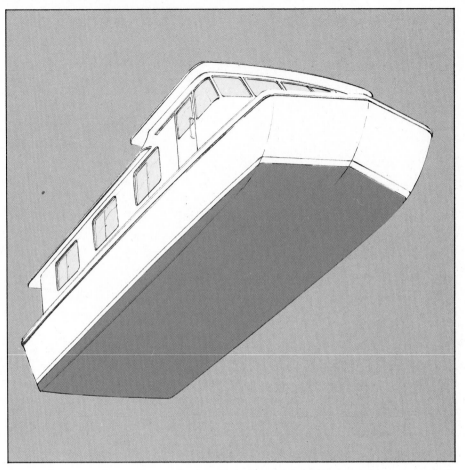

A houseboat's flat-bottomed, straight-sided hull offers minimum wetted surface, making it easy to propel, and maximum beam at the waterline, providing a stable platform. Its construction, moreover, is relatively simple.

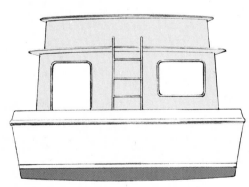

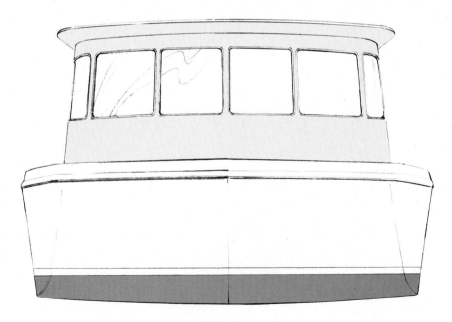

Except for some rudimentary shaping, a flat-bottomed houseboat's bow (above) looks much like its stern (left). The draft is the same fore and aft—as is the very slight deadrise.

The Successful Semi-V

Most of the millions of motorboats on the country's lakes, streams and coastal waters have a hybrid hull called the semi-V. Like all successful designs, it is a compromise—in this instance between the speed and the stability that are offered by flat-bottomed sections and the seaworthiness and comfortable ride that result from a V configuration.

Two advantages of the V shape not shared by the flat bottom are that it cuts into the waves and thus reduces the hull's pounding and that it also acts to give the hull a grip on the water. On the other hand, the V draws more water than a flat bottom does, has greater wetted surface and thus generates more drag. Therefore, many designs combine the virtues of both configurations by joining a pronounced V at the forward end of the hull with a flat planing surface aft. At low speeds and in choppy water, the sharp forward section eases through the waves and keeps the boat moving in a straight line. At high speed in smooth water, the bow lifts out of the water and the boat planes on its wide, flat stern sections.

But even this modification is not perfect. At high speed in rough water, the semi-V's flat sections will pound almost as much as those of the houseboat. And if the vessel is caught out in the open where big waves are overtaking the hull, the wide, buoyant stern tends to ride high while the V-shaped bow digs in. This may initiate a dangerous action that is called broaching, in which the boat lurches sideways to the tumbling seas.

Despite these limitations, however, the semi-V is successful enough to have been adapted to pleasure boats of all sizes from 12 up to 24 feet.

The popular semi-V hull is quite beamy and has considerable stability, particularly when it is planing on its wide after sections. This hull is designed for outboard power, but many semi-Vs are fitted for inboard engines.

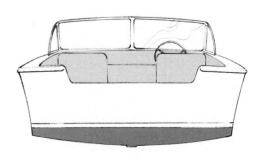

Seen from dead ahead (above), the semi-V hull shows a steep angle of deadrise. Farther aft the V shape decreases gradually until at the stern (right) the bottom is almost flat.

The Deep-Sea Deep V

Although yachtsmen have recently developed a passion for offshore powerboat racing in vessels with deep-V hulls, the bottom shape of these seagoing speedsters is not new. Noah's ark probably had it, and Henry Hudson's *Half Moon* certainly had. Its distinguishing characteristic is a steep angle of deadrise, more than 20°, that carries back for the full length of the hull instead of flattening toward the stern as it does in the semi-V hull. The result is a shape that behaves well at speed in rough water, slicing through heavy waves rather than pounding along on top of them. This is why yacht designer Ray Hunt used it in 1960 to create a 31-foot offshore racer, named *Moppie,* that set off the deep-V phenomenon of recent years.

Like any design, the deep V has limitations. Narrower and deeper than a semi-V or a flat-bottomed hull, it draws more water and tends to roll about more when at rest. Lacking a flat surface, the deep-V hull would have trouble planing were it not for the series of longitudinal ridges, called riding strakes, that are molded into its bottom—and that also serve to deflect spray down and away from the hull, giving them their other name, spray rails.

A great deal of power is required to drive the hull up onto the strakes; and this means bigger and more expensive engines than those commonly used for most boats the same size. But once the deep V gets up, it comes into its own; in heavy going no other hull shape can touch it. The faster the boat goes, the more stable it becomes as it cleaves the waves. It also rights itself particularly well from a roll in heavy seas. This makes it popular not only in ocean racing but for any use that requires speed in rough water, such as sport fishing or water-skiing in open areas.

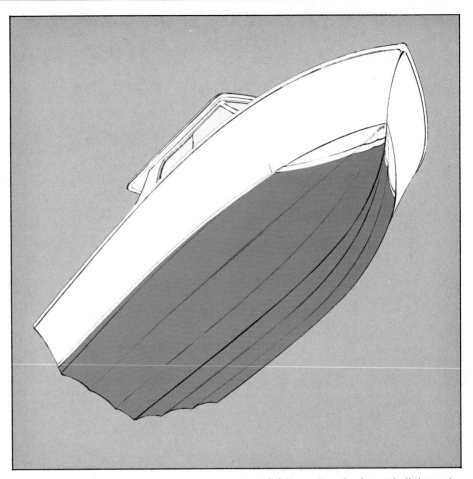

A fish's-eye view of a deep-V hull shows the riding strakes, which provide horizontal planing surfaces. At top speed the hull rides on the innermost pair of strakes; only the small V between them is in the water.

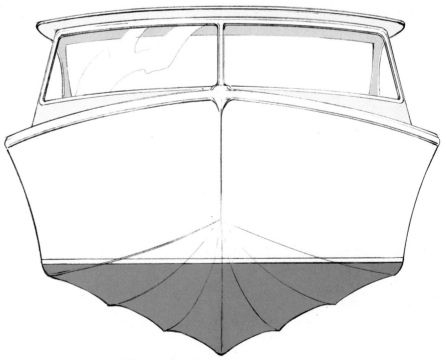

Bow (right) and stern views illustrate how the deep V's relatively steep deadrise carries back to the stern—unlike the semi-V hull, which warps from a V bow to a flat plane aft.

The Complex Cathedral

Turned upside down, the cross section of this complex design bears some resemblance to the roof line of a domed church. But that architectural coincidence hasn't anything to do with the design's name, which, derived from the Greek, simply means angled downward *(kath,* down, plus *hedra,* planes, or plane surfaces that are angled downward). The advantage of this design is that two shallow Vs flanking a deeper central V produce a craft that is stable both at rest and at slow speed. Moreover, it does not have the deep V's tendency to bank too much in a turn.

The adaptability of fiberglass to complex structural forms makes feasible the manufacture of the cathedral hull with its multiple intersecting planes. And indeed most cathedral hulls are made of that material—though some are aluminum. The broadside profile of the cathedral is generally straight; its topsides rise almost vertically from the water and the bow is blunt. As a result, the hull is as steady as a flat bottom at rest and offers just as much usable room on board. In addition, at moderate speeds the cathedral navigates smoothly over choppy water, splitting the waves and not pounding into them.

These advantages make the cathedral hull an excellent design for families that want roominess and comfort and for fishermen and scuba divers who need a stable platform. On the other hand, the cathedral is likely to pound at high speed in rough water and drench its passengers with spray. In addition, the substantial amount of fiberglass used in its construction makes a cathedral costlier than an equal-sized semi-V and also heavier—and that means it needs more power. All this tends to limit the cathedral's popularity to boats under 20 feet long.

The cathedral hull's impressive stability is implicit in the shape of its underside. With most models the side Vs are shallower than the center one and may also be shorter, thus reducing wetted surface and drag.

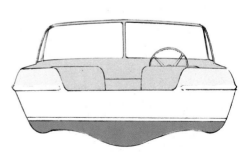

The Vs at the bow of a cathedral hull (left) are sharp for an easy entry into waves, while those at the stern are considerably softer and less pronounced for efficient planing.

The Fast Planing Sportsman

Many cruising and offshore sport-fishing boats are big brothers to the semi-V. That is, their hulls warp from a pronounced-V shape at the bow to a flattish stern. The object of this so-called semidisplacement hull, as with the smaller semi-Vs, is versatility: to combine the maneuverability and sea-kindliness of the V with the get-up-and-go of a planing hull. The compromise serves admirably, for instance, in the sport-fishing boat, which is a vessel with a split personality: it must get out quickly as a planing speedboat to where the fish are, but once out there it should ride the sea gently at slow speeds and not bang into waves and be tossed about by them as a flat-bottomed craft would.

The semidisplacement hull is useful not merely in sport-fishing boats, although they may be the most dashing of the breed. Most of the big cruisers on the nation's waters are variations on the same theme, at least underwater. Therefore besides being fast and seaworthy, the semidisplacement hull must be deep enough to provide room for full living quarters and to accommodate one or two inboard engines. All of these accouterments are heavy, and weight, as well as depth of hull, militates against planing; so a semidisplacement hull needs ample power to get up on its high-speed lines.

Water resistance must also be kept to a minimum. For instance, most planing cruisers have a pronounced chine forward that forms a wide-sweeping bow wave rather than one that rides up along the hull and adds to wetted surface. These deeply angled, sharp-chined bows give semidisplacement vessels a rakish look when clipping along at planing speed. At such speeds they are also likely to cause the hefty wake that has raised the hackles of many a skipper in less sporty craft.

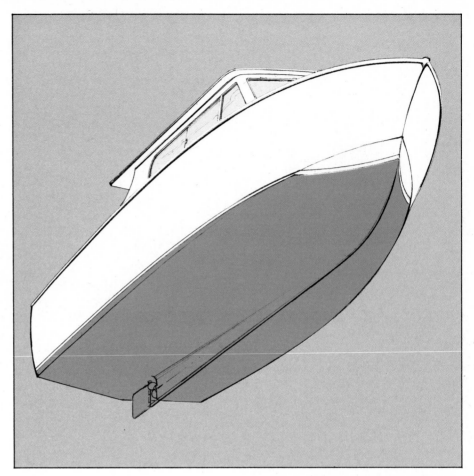

Most semidisplacement hulls have inboard power—a single engine, such as this one, or twin engines—and a skeg to provide lateral resistance and guard prop and rudder.

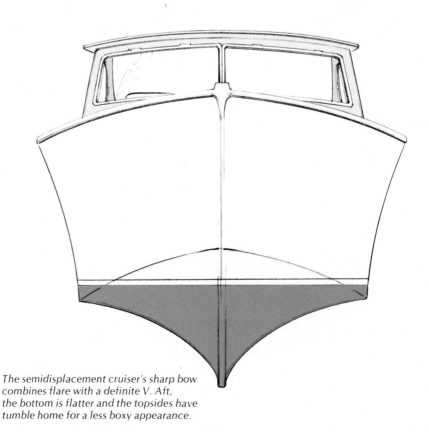

The semidisplacement cruiser's sharp bow combines flare with a definite V. Aft, the bottom is flatter and the topsides have tumble home for a less boxy appearance.

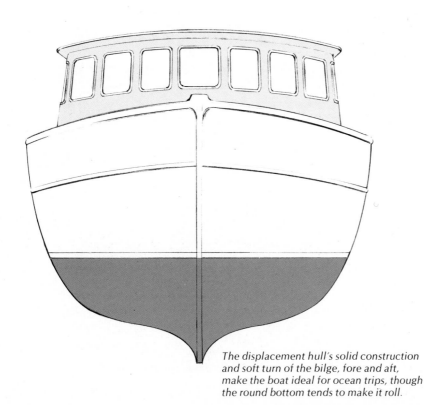

The full-displacement trawler-yacht has a traditional look topside, a bluff bow and no flat surfaces to pound the waves. Though slow, the boat moves easily to hull speed.

A Round-bottomed Cruiser

A growing demand among pleasure boatmen for slow-but-sure cruising comfort has revived interest in the oldest shape of all: the round-bottomed displacement hull. This conformation, the classic shape of commercial fishing vessels, probably descended from the dugout canoes that primitive tribesmen carved for millennia from solid logs. Eskimos give their skin-covered kayaks the same shape. The reason is efficiency: the motive power of canoes and kayaks is paddles and muscles, and round hulls are easier to drive through the water at slow speeds than hulls whose wetted surface is increased by angles and flat planes.

At the end of the last century, the full-displacement, round-bottomed hull was the usual shape for powerboats. But the advent of planing hulls led to a concentration on speed, and in the course of the next half century speedboats and semi-displacement craft came to dominate the pleasure-boat fleet. Then, in the 1960s powerboatmen began to awake to the joys of long-distance cruising; they learned to prize ruggedness and sea-kindliness over speed and dash, and the cult of the so-called trawler-yacht was born.

Named after the rugged trawlers that spend days at a time fishing offshore, the pleasure trawler also is heavy and rugged; and it is ideal for long-distance cruising in fair conditions or foul. Its power plant is usually diesel, which is better geared to slower and heavier going than high-speed gasoline engines and is far more economical over long distances. Under its squarish, traditional-appearing superstructure and in its deep, round bottom, there is generous room for accommodations. It does have a tendency to roll in a heavy sea, but that is a premium paid for its outstanding seaworthiness.

The displacement hull's solid construction and soft turn of the bilge, fore and aft, make the boat ideal for ocean trips, though the round bottom tends to make it roll.

The Comfortable Full Keel

Most powerboats plane, at least partially, but most sailboats do not. To lift a hull of any size onto a plane takes more power than sail alone can usually supply, so the great majority of sailboats are displacement craft. The hull at right is typical of the conventional heavy-displacement designs that have been used for large-boat cruising and ocean racing by several generations of yachtsmen. Its distinguishing feature is a full-bodied underwater section with a fixed keel blending smoothly with the hull's curve and extending downward with generous draft; at the bottom of the keel is a heavy load of ballast, usually lead. Thus the hull's underbody serves admirably to prevent the vessel from sliding sideways while sailing and effectively counters the heeling effect of the wind on the boat's sails.

The ancestry of this modern full-keeler traces directly to a 46-foot yacht named *Gloriana,* built in 1891 by the master designer, Nathanael Herreshoff. In that historic craft, Herreshoff discarded the rectangular, full-length keel and the up-and-down stem of his era's sailing ships; instead, he cut back the forefoot—the area where the stem joins the keel—in a long, gentle curve that eliminated a great deal of wetted surface. This lead to a triangular keel that made *Gloriana's* underbody much deeper aft than forward. In fact, there was hardly a straight line anywhere in her hull—and she simply ran away from the competition.

Boats with essentially the same profile have been cruising and racing on the world's oceans ever since. They are notably seaworthy, with a smooth motion in rough water imparted by the hull's flowing curves, and they are easily held on a steady course through the water. Compared with newer designs, however, such boats tend to be heavy, and despite the sloping forefoot, there is still a lot of wetted surface in their contoured underbodies. Both of these characteristics inhibit speed, so that in competition with the latest racing craft, the full-keeled displacement hull is likely to be a laggard. But for easy handling and long-distance cruising, it is unbeatable.

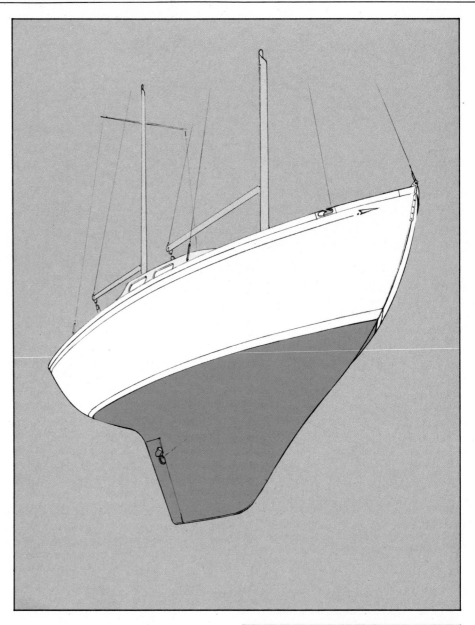

The smooth cutaway curve of the forward edge of this hull's profile is a hallmark of the full-keeled displacement sailboat. Rudder and prop are right behind the keel.

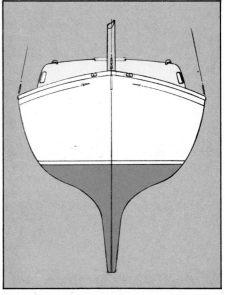

Rounded hull sections and an easy flow of curves from hull to keel contribute to the full-keeled hull's comfortable motion at sea.

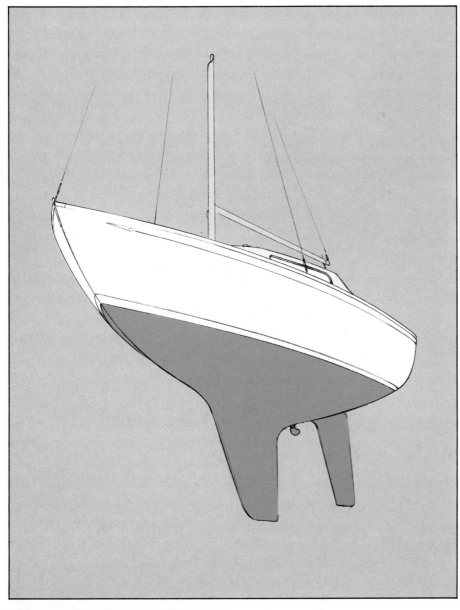

The fin-keeled hull has the least possible underwater surface while still retaining a big enough keel to provide lateral resistance and enough rudder surface to steer the boat.

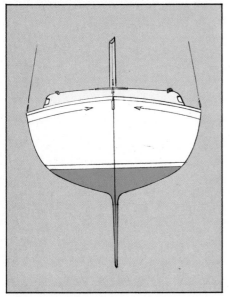

A relatively sharp turn of the bilge, flattish bottom planes and a thin keel are features of a fin-keeled hull designed for speed.

The Lively Fin Keel

The most up-to-date look in seagoing sailboats is the fin-keeled hull—yet there is nothing new about the idea. A familiar example of the fin keel is the 22-foot Star-class racing sloop, which was designed in 1911—and is still going strong with more than 3,000 boats in the class.

What is new in fin-keel design, though, is its application to a host of ocean-racing yachts that not many years ago would have been designed with a fuller, more conventional underbody like the one on the opposite page. The reason for this trend is essentially a matter of taste—the modern yachtsman's appetite for speed.

Almost all of the fin-keeled hull's distinctive features are shaped to reduce wetted surface, since friction against the water is the principal drag on any hull traveling below hull speed. To that end, the keel is short and deep to provide the maximum lateral resistance and a minimum of surface. The rudder is separated from the keel and moved far aft, so that it hangs by itself below the boat's counter. In this position the spade rudder—so called because of its shape—exerts steering leverage more effectively with less surface, producing an instant response that makes the boat agile to the point of skittishness.

The fin-keeled hull also tends to be flatter on the bottom, with more of its fullness pushed up above the waterline. And earnest efforts are made in its design and in its construction to save weight—that is, to keep the displacement of the vessel as light as possible.

All these refinements produce a fast hull—but not without cost. The price is paid primarily in comfort. The lighter, quicker hull is bouncy in a rough sea, and its flattish bottom lines pound more than do the matronly curves of the full-keeled vessel. Furthermore, the diminished underwater profile that makes the boat nimble also makes it more sensitive to the variable forces of wind and wave and calls for constant and expert attention to steering. Nevertheless, the fin-keeled hull is perfectly seaworthy, and many ocean racers gladly put up with its discomforts in return for its speed.

A Versatile Centerboarder

A combination of keel and centerboard—built into the 25-foot sailing cruiser at right—exploits the advantages of both. The abbreviated keel is heavy enough to help the boat resist the heeling force of wind and waves. The lowered centerboard has enough underwater surface to keep the boat from sliding sideways while sailing; with the board up, the keel provides some lateral resistance, and a sailor can navigate safely in shallow water and also load his craft onto a trailer.

Favorites with American designers for a century and a half, the drop-keelers, as they used to be called, sailed in many roles in the 19th Century—as coastal cargo carriers and as some of the biggest, fastest pleasure yachts of the era. In more recent times, a host of successful ocean racers—from 30 to 80 feet long—have combined a keel with centerboard. The board in these seagoing craft is a metal plate weighing anywhere from a few hundred pounds to several tons, rigged with mechanical or hydraulic devices for lowering and raising it. Even so, the board usually weighs less than a ballasted keel does; therefore keel-centerboarders are likely to have more beam than keelboats, gaining from their extra width the stability that would otherwise be provided by weight in a deep keel.

Still more recent is the adaptation of the keel-centerboard concept for trailer-sailers. Fitted with generous living accommodations for their size, these cruisers are not noted for speed, but they get to their weekend destination and back to the car and trailer in reasonable comfort. And as marina space in many parts of the country has become scarcer and more expensive, the popularity of trailer-sailers has skyrocketed. Two decades ago, there was no such thing as live-aboard sailboats that could be hauled about behind the family car; today, there are dozens of models of trailer-sailers in production, and these versatile craft have become the cornerstone of the market for cruising sailboats under 25 feet in length.

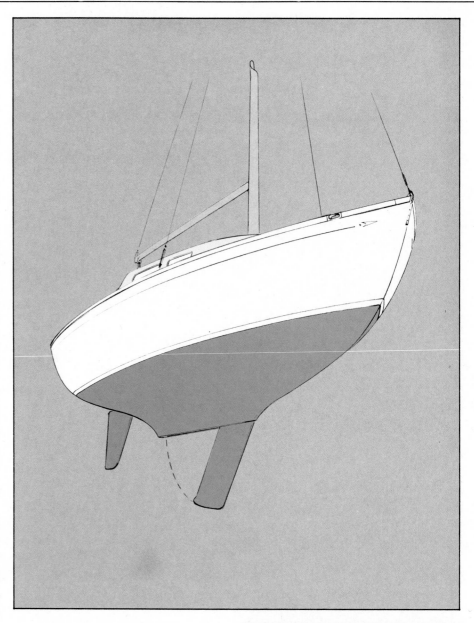

A small keel-centerboarder combines trailability with overnight cruising facilities. The narrow 500-pound steel centerboard swings up inside the stubby keel.

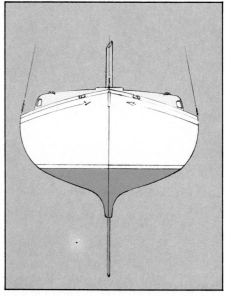

With its board down the keel-centerboarder resembles a fin-keeler; with its board up it draws less than half as much water.

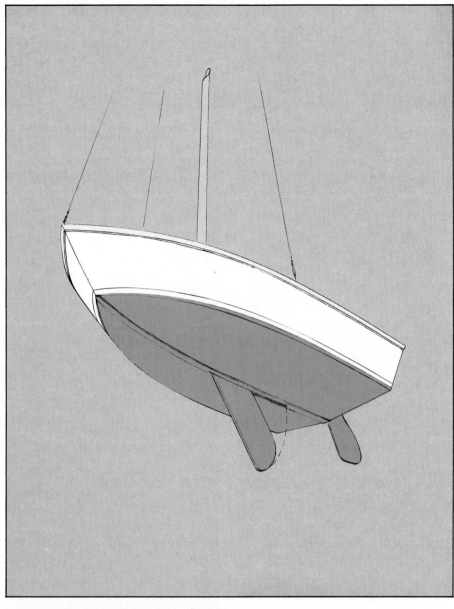

Its centerboard raised into the hull, this small day sailer's bottom is unencumbered except for a small skeg aft, which allows safe beaching and easy trailering.

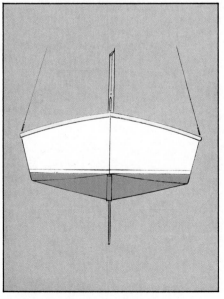

The straight sides and hard chines of this centerboarder make it easy to build, and many such boats are homemade.

The Ubiquitous Day Sailer

Almost everybody learns to sail in small centerboard boats, and these vessels, usually under 20 feet long, are the most numerous of all sailboats. Made of every material and by every technique known to boatbuilding, they come in an endless variety of shapes, sizes and price ranges.

The little boat at left is typical—14 feet of responsive and sporty sailing. The centerboard pivots up into a narrow watertight housing, or trunk, inside the boat. (In some small sailboats the board moves straight up and down and is called a dagger board.) The appeal of such small centerboarders rests on three characteristics: they are usually cheaper to build than keelboats; they are light and easy to handle; and like their bigger cruising cousins, the keel-centerboarders, they can be conveniently mounted on a trailer and towed to the nearest water.

The water need not be deep; a nearly flat-bottomed centerboarder draws only two to three feet with the board down and almost none at all with the board up. The boats are thus ideal for shallow lakes, bays, ponds and tidal estuaries, in which centerboarders can be sailed even at extreme low water.

Underway, small centerboarders make good teachers. With no keel and not much weight in the centerboard—which is usually just a smooth wood board or thin metal plate—the boats are apt to be tippy and lively; skippers and crew find it expedient to learn quickly. Still, there are very few sailors—even experts—who have not tipped over and dumped themselves and their crew in the drink.

Fortunately this usually does no harm. In fact, it is hard to get into serious difficulty in a small centerboarder: lacking heavy keels, they gather little momentum underway and can be banged into docks, buoys and other boats with little harm—except bruised egos.

Because of their low cost and high sportiness, small centerboarders are the ideal boats for one-design class competition—racing in which boats built to identical measurements can race without handicap head to head. There are more than 250 classes of centerboarders racing in the United States alone, ranging in sophistication from snub-nosed prams to Olympic-class planing hulls.

For Speed: Planing Hulls

Though planing sailboats are less numerous than conventional displacement vessels, more are being built to satisfy a growing demand among sailors for the thrills of speed. The key features of a planing boat are lightness, a flat bottom and enough sail area to generate the power needed to get the hull up and planing.

Since the prime object of planing sailboats is exciting sport, it is not surprising that virtually all such craft belong to various one-design racing classes. Their increasing popularity is shown by the fact that four of the six Olympic-class boats are planing craft: the single-handed 15-foot Finn, the 15½-foot 470, the 20-foot Flying Dutchman—all centerboarders—and the 22-foot fin-keeled Tempest.

But the planing sailboat is by no means a modern development. Since the end of the last century a group of keenly competitive planing classes known collectively as scows have demanded highly developed skills from an ardent following of sailors, mostly in the Great Lakes region but more recently in many other parts of the country that offer sheltered waters. The scow is a distinctive-looking craft *(right)*. Besides the square bow and the shallow draft that led to its decidedly inappropriate name, it is unique among single-hulled sailboats in sporting on each side a rudder and an angled centerboard, or bilge board; each pair comes into play in turn as the boat heels to one side and then the other. The largest scow, the A class, measures 38 feet, while the little M scow is only 16 feet, but all are fast sailers—"A"s have gone over 30 miles per hour.

The secret of the scow's speed, as it is for most planing craft, is a minimum of wetted surface and generous sail area. When it is planing, far more of its hull is out of the water than is in it, and the wave-making resistance that limits a displacement hull is virtually eliminated. This produces speed, but it also makes for a finely balanced, high-spirited boat that needs a spry crew and competent skipper.

Related to scows in the family of planing boats—but of less radical design—are the so-called board boats, such as the little Sunfish and Laser. Simplicity of construction and ease of handling are chiefly responsible for their wide popularity; but the fact that the surfboard-like planing hulls also go very fast—they can reach a speed of 15 miles per hour—is a large part of their appeal. More than a quarter of a million board boats are in use today—ample proof that planing is as much fun as the word suggests it might be.

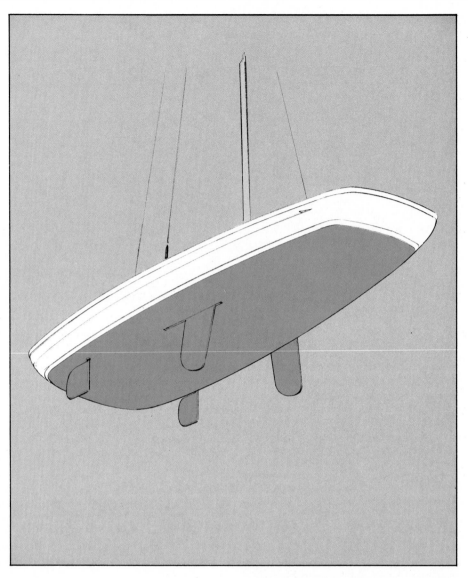

The pivoting bilge boards and double rudders of the scow are angled so that whenever it is sailing heeled over, one pair is efficiently pointing down; the other is out of water.

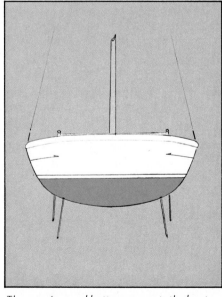

The scow's round bottom presents the least possible surface to the water, a hull shape sometimes called a skimming dish.

For Speed: Multihulls

For centuries the intrepid navigators of the South Seas have used multiple-hulled sailing craft because they are fast, well balanced and easy to build. The same factors help to explain the popularity of the modern twin-hulled catamaran (a term derived from the Tamil tongue of southern India, in which the word *kattumaram* literally means trees tied together) and the triple-hulled trimaran.

The broad base formed by multihulls' wide configuration makes it possible for them to carry an amount of sail that would capsize single hulls of the same size and weight—but that makes the multihulled craft go faster. In recent years multihulls of various types have set records in almost every kind of sailing, from transoceanic runs to out-and-out speed trials *(page 57)*. Because lightness, combined with large sail areas, makes these craft so fast, it was the introduction of strong, lightweight materials—plywood and fiberglass—that spurred the success of modern multihulls.

Though most catamarans have a centerboard in each symmetrical hull to resist sideslip, some haven't even that friction-creating surface. Instead, the hulls are asymmetrical, each having a nearly vertical outboard side that prevents sliding. The trimaran, on the other hand, generally has a keel or centerboard on its center hull, which is shaped something like conventional hulls but is shallower. The two smaller outriding hulls keep a trimaran upright in practically any conditions, and it is in ocean-racing and cruising craft that the design has shown to best advantage.

The drawbacks of multihulls are related to their virtues: steadier than single hulls, they are at the same time more difficult to maneuver; harder to capsize, they are much harder to right when they do. Furthermore, although many multihull designs—lacking complex curves—are easy to build, they are also subject to great stresses because when moving at high speed they are wracked by the twisting and snapping motions their separate hulls make as they go through the water. As a result, many improperly built multihulls have simply come apart in rough conditions. Nevertheless, improved designs grow more popular and multihulls go on increasing their speeds.

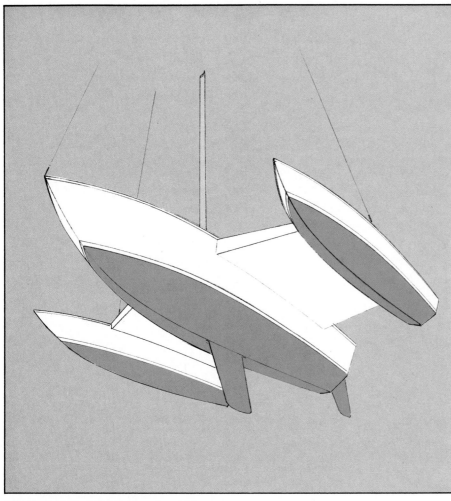

The width of the cruising trimaran, with its flanking hulls, makes it almost uncapsizable. Weight is largely in the center hull, which holds most of the accommodations.

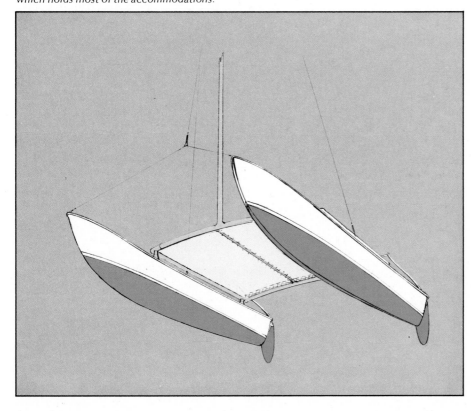

The two hulls of this 14-foot day-sailing catamaran are joined by light, strong aluminum tubing, and the space between them is bridged by a fabric trampoline.

The Search for Stability

In nautical terms, stability is a boat's resistance to being heeled over. For a sailboat, stability is crucial because the wind that propels the boat also tends to tip it. Only by resisting this heeling force can the sailboat convert the wind's pressure into forward motion; the more wind force the boat can withstand without tipping over, the faster it can go.

Two design elements are chiefly responsible for stability. One is a wide, or beamy, hull; the other is weight, or ballast, down in the vessel's keel. Whichever is used, a properly designed boat will have a strong tendency to return to vertical. Physically, this tendency is the product of two opposing forces, gravity and buoyancy. Their interaction is demonstrated at right with three kinds of sailboat hulls.

Theoretically the downward force of gravity acts through a point called the center of gravity (abbreviated as CG); buoyancy's upward thrust acts through the center of buoyancy (CB). When a hull is level, these centers are aligned vertically. When the craft heels, the CB moves toward the lower side and the vertical lines of gravity and buoyancy separate. The distance between those lines is a measure of buoyancy's power to set the hull upright. This distance is called the righting arm, and the longer it is, the more the hull is resisting being heeled.

Each of the hull types is shown heeling at 10°, 35° and 55° as it is pushed by progressively stronger wind pressure. In the first sequence, showing an unballasted, slightly top-heavy hull, the CB moves appreciably toward the low side, even at 10°, producing a considerable righting arm at that slight heel. At 35°, though, the righting arm has started to shrink, and at 55° the lines of buoyancy and gravity are too close for safety: when the CG passes over the CB, the hull will capsize.

The deep hull in the middle row gets stability from the ballast in its keel. This gives it little resistance to heeling at 10°, but the more it heels and the higher its weighted keel is raised, the greater the vessel's righting arm becomes. The hull thus is virtually uncapsizable.

The catamaran (bottom row) represents an extreme in beaminess, which gives it tremendous initial stability. This stability holds until the craft reaches a critical angle of heel; then its righting arm plummets to zero, and the boat keeps going over.

One added factor can help avert this calamity; that is the use of movable ballast, or crew weight. This element of stability is illustrated on pages 56 and 57.

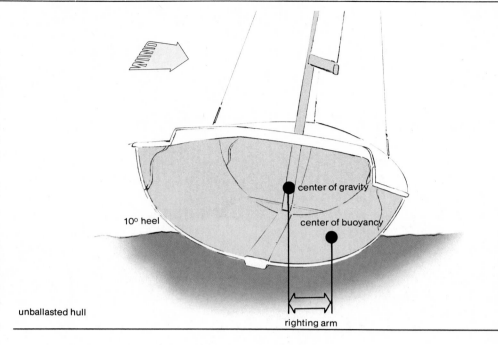

10° heel

center of gravity

center of buoyancy

righting arm

unballasted hull

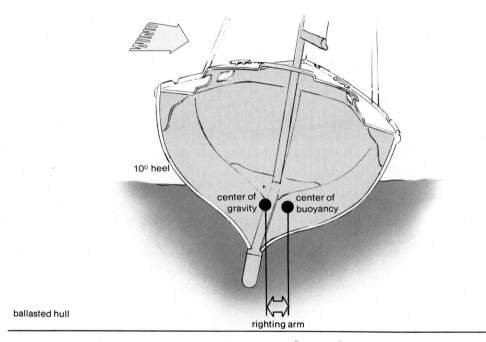

10° heel

center of gravity

center of buoyancy

righting arm

ballasted hull

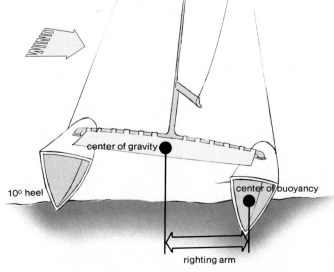

10° heel

center of gravity

center of buoyancy

righting arm

catamaran

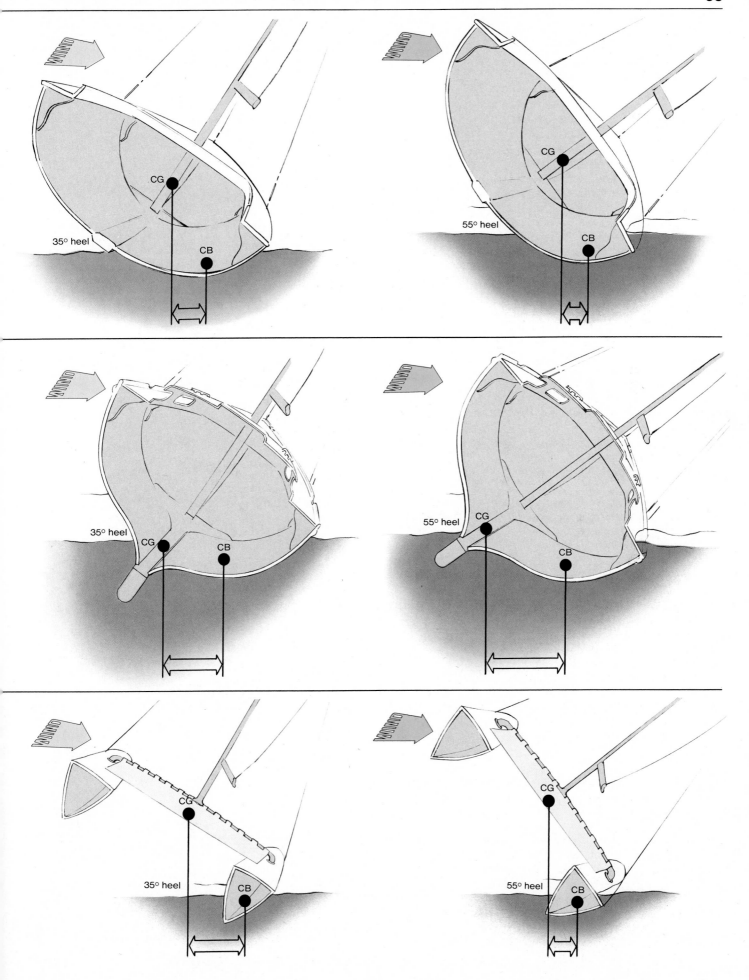

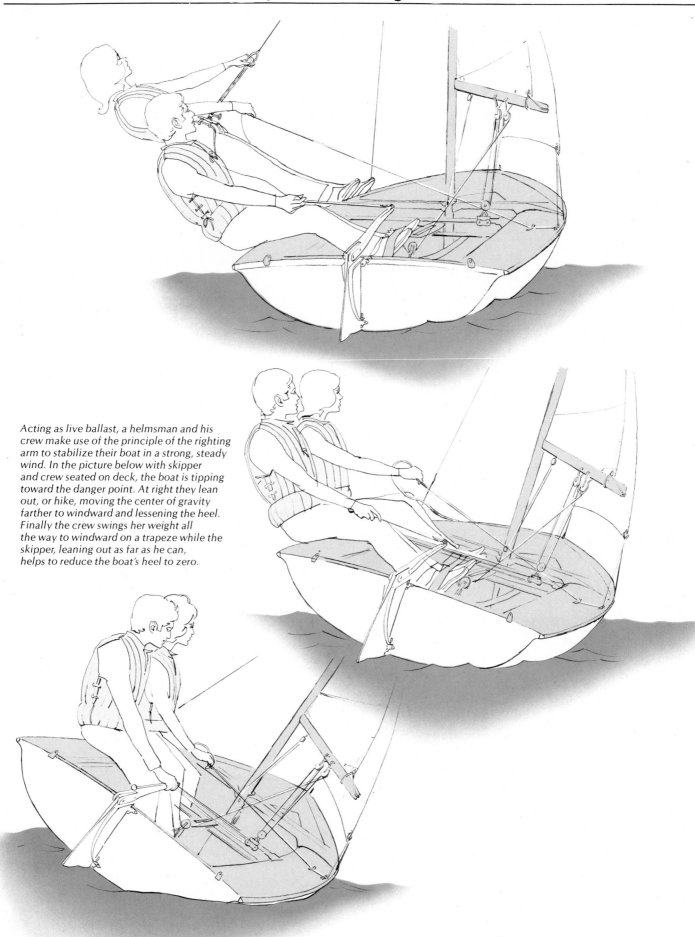

Acting as live ballast, a helmsman and his crew make use of the principle of the righting arm to stabilize their boat in a strong, steady wind. In the picture below with skipper and crew seated on deck, the boat is tipping toward the danger point. At right they lean out, or hike, moving the center of gravity farther to windward and lessening the heel. Finally the crew swings her weight all the way to windward on a trapeze while the skipper, leaning out as far as he can, helps to reduce the boat's heel to zero.

A Far-out Design for Stability

The righting arm to end all righting arms is that of the English vessel *Crossbow,* an ultra-sophisticated version of a multihull called a proa. Where other proas have a simple float connected to a larger hull by a pair of arms, in the manner of the Indonesian outrigger canoe that inspired the design, 60-foot *Crossbow* has an auxiliary hull 25 feet out. Assisted out of the water by a hydrofoil, the smaller hull holds its crew members airborne; their weight stabilizes almost 1,000 square feet of sail. *Crossbow's* exotic rig permits her to sail only with the wind over her left side. She was not designed for maneuverability, however, but for speed: in 1973 she set a speed record by averaging 33 mph over a measured course.

THE CHEERFUL EARLY DAYS OF BOATING

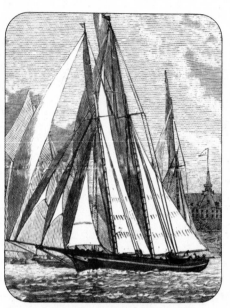

Flying all her sails, a New York Yacht Club schooner races up Long Island Sound in 1878.

In most people's minds, American yachting during its early days was a sport for millionaires. And small wonder. Shipping magnate George Crowninshield, who owned the first United States pleasure yacht of record, splurged an extravagant $50,000 in 1816 to build his 100-foot *Cleopatra's Barge* and furnish it with gilded mirrors, a chandelier and velvet-covered lines. Five decades later, the high-rolling membership of the New York Yacht Club raced majestic schooners like the one at right for purses that ran as high as $60,000.

Yet even as the rich tried to outdazzle one another with the luxury or speed of their vessels, ordinary Americans of the mid-19th Century began making a modest splash of their own.

At first, these new yachtsmen sailed in adapted working craft, such as fishing smacks and oyster boats. But soon new varieties of craft evolved, designed simply for pleasure. One extremely popular small boat of the era was the sailing canoe, conceived by an Englishman named John MacGregor in 1865. MacGregor liked his canoe so much that he designed it to fit inside a railroad car so he could take it with him when he traveled. Thousands of others liked the sailing canoe, too *(page 64)*. In the 1870s and 1880s they paddled or sailed their way to so-called canoe encampments where they would race, wager and generally whoop it up.

Primitive powerboats brought another breed of enthusiast to the water, lured by the speed and excitement of the new steam-, electric- and naptha-powered engines. In 1854 an enterprising 13-year-old designer from Staten Island, New York, built a steam launch that he fueled with his father's whiskey.

Most steam engines in those wacky, adventurous early days were fired by huge amounts of coal or wood. Often the fuel ran out in mid-voyage, with the result that anything burnable got thrown in the firebox. As one disgruntled motorboatman put it, the craft "usually arrives home minus seats, lockers and floor boards."

But nothing daunted these early boatmen. The ladies were just as enthusiastic, encumbered though they were by corsets, crinolines and muttonchop sleeves—and, occasionally, by the ancient male prejudice against women at sea. After an 1890 rowboat accident involving a squadron of seagoing ladies, the Buffalo *Express* sternly laid down the following rules: "Don't take more than six women out when the water is rough. Don't take six women out when the water isn't rough. Don't take any women out in either case."

In spite of such mishaps and grouchy reflections, pleasure boating caught on as good, healthy fun for everyone. One new boatowner of the 1880s summed up the general mood: "Before, I was constantly suffering from dyspepsia and other troubles arising from too close attention to business. Now I am a well man."

Proud and happy members of yachting's new class muster around the mast of their catboat before setting out for an afternoon sail in 1891.

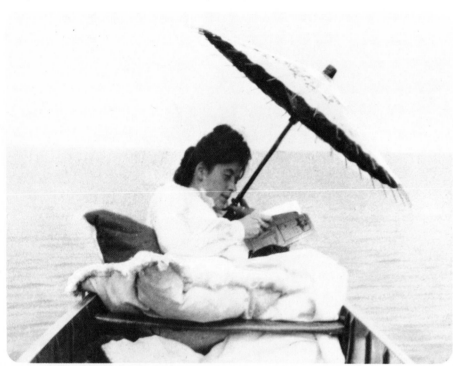

Peacefully ensconced in the bow of a rowboat with book and parasol, a 19th Century lady enjoys the simple pleasures of a calm, sunny day on the water.

A busy afternoon at White Bear Yacht Club near St. Paul, Minnesota, brings together a mixed fleet of motor launches and windjammers. The sailing craft are recognizable ancestors of modern inland-racing scows—but the lady sailors of the day are distinctly overcanvased.

A flotilla of rowboats drifts gently downstream on the Wisconsin River in the 1880s. The top-hatted oarsmen and their lady passengers, some reclining in armchairs mounted astern, were ferried upriver in a steamboat so no one had to row against the current.

A matronly aquanaut takes her cat for a ride in a lapstrake rowboat—possibly one built at home. As early as 1876 pioneer yachting publications were giving detailed instructions on do-it-yourself boatbuilding.

Pleasure-boaters on a Minnesota lake come together for an impromptu gam—the nautical term for a congregation of boats at sea.

Combining the two most popular sporting
fads of the day—boats and bicycles—
this improbable craft needed two makeshift
outriggers simply to stay upright and
a lot of pedaling to go anywhere at all.

Two-masted sailing canoes like this one
tipped over so easily that sliding seats were
devised in the 1890s to allow helmsmen
to shift their weight out beyond the rail
as a counterbalance to the wind's pressure.

A wonderfully complex craft, with twin bowsprits and dual outriggers, skims across the water at Sausalito, California, guided by a skipper in a stovepipe hat. Such speedy, multihulled sailboats won so many races that rival yachtsmen tried to ban them from competition.

A nattily dressed fisherman aboard the steam launch Unidilla
shows off a mammoth muskellunge he has just caught in Long Lake,
Wisconsin. The wood pile provided fuel for the engine, and the
rack lashed beneath the owl figurehead was used for hauling ice.

The owner of an electric-powered paddle wheeler poles down the Gasconade River in Missouri after his exotic craft ran out of juice. To recharge the batteries each time they expired, he had to plug in to a shore generator—or he could hook up to a power line or the live rail of a streetcar track.

A cheerful party of semisubmerged sailors—
including a diehard helmsman and an
umbrella-wielding crew member—hams it up
for the camera on Minnesota's White Bear
Lake. Despite their tippiness, sailing scows
like this were highly popular on inland lakes
in the 1890s—and remain so today.

A racing sloop ghosts to a landing at the end of a day's sail on Grand Lake, Colorado, in the middle of the Rocky Mountains, nearly two miles above sea level and 1,000 miles from the nearest coast.

3 There seems almost no end to the imagination and ingenuity brought forth in men by the challenge of building boats. Irish seafarers during Europe's Dark Ages explored the North Atlantic in boats of skins stretched over a frame of wood. In one of the Greek sagas, Hercules sailed off to the garden of the Hesperides, at the westernmost edge of the world, in an enormous clay pot. Today hulls of steel monopolize the world's commercial shipping lanes, and a few steel boats appear in yacht marinas. For the most part, however, the waterways of the United States and Europe are filled with pleasure craft created from four very dissimilar but equally remarkable materials: wood, fiberglass,

HOW BOATS ARE BUILT

ferro-cement and, as in the case of the racing sloop at left, aluminum. Each has its own special advantages for boatbuilding—and its own unique structural properties that require particular building techniques.

Traditionally, shipbuilders have used wood whenever it was available—to the extent of causing its scarcity. A thick forest would still cover northern Morocco had not Roman shipbuilders, and later the Spanish, cut down most of the trees to construct their imperial fleets. England sacrificed its ancient stands of oak to build the Royal Navy. Wood for boatbuilding is now scarce the world over. No more than 5 to 10 per cent of today's pleasure craft are being made from wood, compared with 85 per cent just a few decades ago. And though part of the change is caused by the high cost of handcrafting, a major factor is the difficulty of coming by good, seasoned timber.

Many yachtsmen consider this trend away from wood construction to be one of the more lamentable facts of modern life. Granted, wooden hulls have certain innate shortcomings—they leak at the joints, they rot, they play host to various kinds of marine growths, and the cost of maintaining them sometimes threatens to pauperize their owners. But for some people, there is just no substitute for the rich sheen of varnished mahogany, the feel of a teak deck underfoot, the comforting solidity of oak timbers or even for the special sound that water makes as it laps against a wooden hull.

The basic methods for constructing wooden boats have changed so little over the centuries that a shipwright from 17th Century Amsterdam would have no trouble finding work in one of the present-day boatyards that continue to build wooden yachts. He would recognize each time-proven step, from the laying of a keel to the final smoothing and fairing of the completed hull. He would know the merits of the carefully selected woods that modern shipwrights still use. Teak, for example, contains an oil that keeps out moisture and thus guards against rot. White oak is so tough and pliable that, after being immersed in steam, it can literally be tied into knots—a characteristic that allows it to be shaped into the curved frames of the hull.

But as teak and oak and other fine hardwoods become increasingly scarce, and the skills of good ships' carpenters grow ever more expensive, boatbuilders are turning to other materials. One of the most unlikely of these is ferro-cement, a substance utterly lacking in nautical tradition—unless Hercules' pot provides some sort of historical precedent. Ferro-cement made its nautical debut during the early 1940s when the Italian architect Luigi Nervi, already a master of reinforced concrete for autobahns and airdromes, turned his talents to boat design. Nervi developed a method for impregnating multiple layers of steel mesh with cement to form a shell that was light and thin enough to be buoyant. With it he built himself a 165-ton ferro-cement motor sailer that chugged impressively around the Mediterranean for more than a decade with almost no hull maintenance.

Not all the successors to Nervi's boat are so trouble free, particularly since

The gleaming aluminum hull of a 12-meter racing yacht, polished and painted, rolls from the shed where it was built. It will now be given an aluminum mast and steel rigging.

a high percentage of such craft are built by backyard amateurs *(pages 80-81)* rather than by professionals wise in the ways of ferro-cement. Nevertheless, the material has its admirers, primarily because of a toughness that seems almost legendary. One Canadian builder of commercial fishing vessels smashed his 42-foot cement trawler into a reef—and bounced right through it. The vessel suffered no more damage than a scrape along its bottom. But the top of the reef was sheared right off, rocks, oysters and all.

In common with some other modern boatbuilding materials, ferro-cement frees shipwrights from many of the ancient strictures of boat construction and allows them to operate with a totally new and simplified approach. In a traditional wooden boat, most of the stress is carried by an interior framework of ribs and beams, while rows of exterior planking, attached to the framework, act like a skin to keep out the water. But with ferro-cement and such other materials as molded plywood and fiberglass, the exterior skin is strong enough to provide its own support, with no interior framework needed. The hull is, in effect, a monolithic shell, without seams or joints.

The substance that most fully exploits the potential of this shell construction is fiberglass. A fiberglass hull is fashioned from multiple laminations of fiberglass cloth that are shaped inside a mold and then fused with a gluelike binder of hard-setting plastic resin. The process is a quick one. The resulting hull is both strong and sleek. And the construction method is simple enough to be accomplished by semiskilled labor. Indeed, glass boats can be produced with such assembly-line dispatch that they have come to dominate the new-boat market. According to one estimate, during the early 1970s they accounted for 93 per cent of all new-yacht sales.

Some boatowners, nostalgic about the beauties of wood, complain that fiberglass craft smell of resin, are unpleasantly noisy underway and lack character or distinction. And it is a fact that most glass boats are production models, identical in every detail down to the last molded-in wine rack.

But because of the tremendous number of boats that come off these standardized production lines, more people than ever before have been able to experience the joys of yachting. Not only are fiberglass hulls easy to build, they are as easy to maintain as any boat can be. There is no need each spring to scrape down, recaulk or recarpenter a fiberglass bottom, as must be done with wood. Instead, an annual application of automobile wax is often sufficient to ready the hull for launching.

The most serious challenger to fiberglass as a modern boatbuilding material is aluminum. Small skiffs and rowboats have been made from aluminum for decades, and even as early as the 1890s a few venturesome Europeans were sailing around in experimental aluminum hulls. But pure aluminum, while fine for small craft, is not strong enough for large vessels. It must be alloyed with another metal to toughen it. For many years, however, no one could find an aluminum alloy that did not suffer ruinously from corrosion.

All metals corrode to some degree, particularly in salt water. The problem is exacerbated when two metals are combined—when a hull of steel, for example, contains fittings and fastenings of bronze, or when the wrong metals are used as alloys. An electrochemical action develops, with the metals acting like the two poles of a storage battery, that can disintegrate a boat as surely as termites can eat away a house. And this is precisely what happened with hulls made from the first aluminum alloys; they simply dissolved under the dismayed eyes of their owners.

The problem was solved in 1931, when metallurgists developed a combination of aluminum and magnesium that was—and is—almost corrosion free. Outboard boatbuilders were the first to use the new alloy for quantity production. But aluminum did not really come into its own until the early 1960s, when large aluminum sailing boats began running away with some top racing trophies. The Chicago to Mackinac race, the Newport to Bermuda, the San Diego to Acapulco, all fell to aluminum craft. And now, for many yachtsmen it appears that aluminum will be the stuff of the future.

A Critique of Construction Materials

	Wood	Fiberglass	Ferro-Cement	Aluminum and Steel
Initial Cost	Prices of seasoned timber are high, and the cost of skilled labor even higher. A cheaper alternative, particularly for small boats, is marine plywood—either used instead of conventional planking over an inner framework, or nailed or screwed together in flat sections, or else bent to shape over a mold.	The raw materials—fiberglass and polyester or epoxy resin—are even more expensive than wood. But production-line methods drive down construction costs and make the price of most fiberglass boats attractive.	Cement is the cheapest of all boatbuilding substances and a favorite of amateur shipwrights. But though the cost of materials is low, the number of man-hours needed to assemble them into a boat is high, representing a major investment of an amateur boatbuilder's time.	Aluminum is expensive and so, too, is the skilled labor needed to cut, fit and shape it. But in mass-produced small boats and custom-built yachts of 45 feet or more, its cost is comparable to fiberglass. Steel is cheaper than aluminum, but weighs three times as much.
Maintenance	Annual painting is required to protect the hull and topsides from marine growth and weathering. Screws fastening planks to structural members may deteriorate and need replacing. Periodically the bottom should be scraped down to bare wood, recaulked and restopped with marine putty.	Though easier to maintain than wood, fiberglass boats need a yearly cleaning and waxing and—if kept in salt water—antifouling bottom paint to repel marine growth. The outer surface, or gel coat, is easily marred and its color fades in sunlight, so fiberglass boats should be stored indoors or under a tarpaulin.	Surface paint must be renewed periodically to prevent the cement from absorbing water, which could penetrate to the interior metal framework and rust it. Chips in the cement surface should be filled with polyester compound, and all fittings should be checked for signs of corrosion.	A major maintenance problem with both steel and aluminum boats is protecting them from corrosion. Steel is more vulnerable, especially to rust, and must always be protected by paint. Aluminum does not rust, but its surface may corrode and become pitted from exposure to salt water.
Sturdiness	Wood is strong and resilient and on impact tends to give slightly, then spring back. But a major collision will rupture a wooden hull, causing it to splinter extensively around the point of impact.	Fiberglass is one of the strongest boatbuilding materials and can absorb powerful impacts before fracturing. When it does fracture, cracks may radiate well beyond the contact point, and the layers of fiberglass may begin to delaminate, or come apart, seriously weakening the entire hull.	Impact on a ferro-cement hull causes less extensive injury than to wood or fiberglass. Ferro-cement is likely to pulverize at the point of contact rather than fracture or splinter across a wide area of the hull.	Aluminum is stronger for its weight than any other boatbuilding material, but when used in thin plates for a boat's hull, it is vulnerable to denting. Steel, though heavier, is also tremendously strong and, like aluminum, is more likely to dent than fracture or puncture on impact.
Repairs	Even minor work requires a fair degree of carpentry skill. Damaged planks or plywood sections must be removed and new ones fitted. Damage to the interior hull framework may require major surgery at a boatyard.	Injury to the gel coat is fixed by filling with epoxy putty and refinishing. Punctures in fiberglass are repaired by cutting out the damaged area and rebuilding it with layers of fiberglass material cemented in place with polyester resin—a job well within the capability of a handy amateur.	No material is easier to fix than ferro-cement. In repairing a damaged hull, the loose cement is knocked away, the internal metalwork reshaped or replaced and the opening filled with fresh mortar.	Minor dents can be hammered out with a rubber mallet. More extensive damage is quickly repaired by cutting and welding—a job usually done at a boatyard.
Remarks	Except for small plywood craft, very few stock wood boats are now produced. A wood boat is usually built to order—either overseas or at a few traditional boatyards in New England, on Chesapeake Bay and on the West Coast. Sound wood vessels may still be found in the used-boat market (pages 134-137).	Although fiberglass boats are impervious to the organic decay that afflicts wood, the material is still too new for its life span to have been tested. Hulls are virtually leakproof, but poor joints between deck and hull may cause trouble. Critics complain of a resin smell and the material's plastic appearance.	Problems of ferro-cement construction include rusting of the metal skeleton, peeling and blistering of the finish, and difficulty in getting a smooth, even surface. The heaviness of ferro-cement makes it more suitable to powerboats, workboats or cruising sailboats than to racers.	Aluminum has long been used in canoes and small boats and is now gaining favor with designers of medium to large racing sailboats. Steel is not popular with competitive yachtsmen because of its weight, but its strength and cheapness make it practical for large cruising yachts.

Wood: Classic and Rare

A well-built wooden boat is a remarkable piece of work. Its raw materials may come from all quarters of the globe: teak from Burma for its decks, Philippine mahogany for its hull, Sitka spruce from the American Northwest for the masts and spars. Its parts must be shaped and joined as carefully as fine cabinetry, yet must be rugged enough to withstand battering waves that would knock the wall off a house.

The boatbuilder's art has been perfected through centuries of experience, but in the Western Hemisphere today shipwrights who work in wood are becoming as rare as village blacksmiths. Few large United States boatyards can afford the time and labor costs of building in wood; it took almost half a year to put together each of the ocean-going trawlers at right, for example. Therefore, a skipper attracted by the natural beauty of wood looks overseas to boatyards such as American Marine in Hong Kong, which turns out yachts using the time-honored methods shown on the following pages.

The initial step in building a wooden boat is laying the keel. This essential member, the backbone of the hull, is usually a piece of carefully shaped white oak or fir. To it are attached, first, the stem, an upward-sloping member that forms the bow, and then the various elements that make up the stern. Next come the frames, a series of roughly U-shaped timbers that rise up from the keel like ribs in a skeleton. Transverse beams, which join the opposite sides of each frame, stiffen the ribs and help support the deck; other reinforcing members, called stringers, run lengthwise inside the frames.

Outside this skeleton goes the boat's skin, horizontal rows of closely fitting mahogany planks. Now the boat's interior structure is built in, with particular care taken on the cabin walls—called bulkheads—which add still more strength to the hull. Finally the decks are laid down and hatches and deck houses added.

Each step in this process is exacting and time consuming. Almost every joint must be notched and fitted. Since hulls have few straight lines, almost every strip of wood must be shaped into a curve—always following the natural grain of the wood for strength. To keep hull and deck planking smooth, each screw must be countersunk and covered with a wood plug. Every seam must be made watertight. Only such painstaking craftsmanship will produce a boat tight enough to stay dry inside and sturdy enough to withstand the buffeting of angry seas.

Brand new ocean-going trawler-yachts, displaying the elegance and sturdiness of traditional wood construction, lie moored alongside the Hong Kong boatyard where they were built. These wooden boats require such painstaking workmanship that it takes 1,000 master shipwrights, apprentices and helpers to turn out 120 of them a year.

Surrounded by tiers of scaffolding, craftsmen get ready to lay the keel of a new 48-foot ocean trawler while work continues on several other vessels in the background.

With an adze, one of the oldest of all woodcrafting tools, a shipwright chips away at the timber that will become a vessel's finely tapered stem. Later he will smooth out the surface with an electric sander.

Standing under the forward rise of a newly laid keel, a carpenter prepares to bolt together two notched wooden components— a joining technique called scarfing.

Every surface of a wooden boat must be individually shaped and smoothed, a task this workman performs on a new keel with an electric plane. The keel has been carved from a single piece of a particularly hard wood, called yacal, that comes from Borneo.

With deft handling of hammer and chisel, a workman puts a notch at the bottom of a frame assembly so that it can be fitted to the keel. The piece he is cutting is a short connecting member, called a floor, through which the keel bolts will actually run.

Carefully spaced rows of frames, joined by horizontal deck beams, define the midship skeletons of two 53-foot trawlers; the carpenter in the foreground drills holes in a boat's keel for bolting on the bow frames.

The wooden components in a boat's interior fit together like the pieces of a three-dimensional puzzle. Here workmen assemble teak cabin appointments, including a double bunk with bureau drawers for storage.

Only two weeks away from launching, a 48-foot power cruiser gets a
coat of varnish on its transom while carpenters finish off its deck.
Planks for the decking have been fastened down with bronze screws,
countersunk to one third the plank thickness. The men on deck
drive in plugs to fill the holes, making sure the grain in each plug
runs parallel with that of the planking. After a plug has been tapped
home, its top is lopped off flush to the deck with a chisel.

Bristling with uncut plugs, a trawler's hull awaits caulking—a process in which cotton fibers and sealant are squeezed into the seams between planks to keep out the water.

In a final step toward finishing another pleasure trawler, a workman prepares to weld a life rail in place. When launched, the boat will join its sisters moored in the background, waiting for transport by ship to the U.S.

Cement: Simple and Strong

To most people, the notion of going down to the sea in cement means a trip to the bottom of the harbor in a pair of concrete galoshes. The very idea of cement floating seems an outrageous paradox.

Yet cement boats float very well indeed, and have a reputation for being strong, durable and cheap. Their basic structure, as indicated in the photographs at right, is a thin, tough cement shell reinforced by steel rods and wire mesh—a combination known as ferro-cement. While such hulls are time consuming to build (they take about three times as long as a comparable one made of wood), the techniques are simple enough that a fair number of yachtsmen have successfully fabricated their own concrete yachts.

The most popular construction method begins with the fashioning of a wooden mold over which the hull will be shaped. The boatbuilder covers the mold with several layers of wire mesh, followed by a series of closely spaced steel rods. He then adds more mesh until he has completed a skeleton hull, as shown at the top of the opposite page.

This stage will take the typical amateur builder many months of patient work. But the next step, covering the skeleton with cement, must be accomplished in a single day so that there will be no seams to weaken the hull. The cement has to be forced through the mesh, thoroughly impregnating the skeleton, in order to minimize air pockets—a potential source of leaks. A second pass with the trowel fills in low spots and smooths out humps. The result is a seamless ferro-cement shell about three quarters of an inch thick.

Once formed, the hull must be kept wetted down for at least 28 days so that the cement will harden properly. Then the boatbuilder, using a crane, turns the hull right side up; he rips out the wooden mold, finishes the interior and adds decks and superstructure. The result is a vessel of which any skipper can be proud.

No matter how carefully he has built, the owner of a cement yacht knows he has sacrificed certain advantages. His hull is almost twice as heavy as a comparable one of wood or fiberglass, and its surface is not as smooth. Critics of cement also claim that he has not really saved much money, since the hull normally represents only 10 to 25 per cent of a boat's price tag. But the skipper also knows his yacht is exceptionally strong and damage resistant—and that if he ever does bash it up he can patch it himself with a little wire mesh and a bucket of cement.

A willing crew of neighbors hurries to cement the hull of a 36-foot ketch. The owner, a Massachusetts yachtsman, recruited 24 hands, who worked steadily for 16 hours, using 36 bags of cement and more than two tons of sand. The hull took more than 15 months to construct, but the total cost of materials came to only $970.

Awaiting mortar, the wire-mesh skeleton of a 34-foot ketch encloses the wood mold that was used to shape it. A boat of this size may require some 4,000 square feet of mesh.

The finished hull of a 49-foot ferro-cement ketch stands ready in a Maryland boatyard to receive its interior fittings — to be followed by its first coat of paint. Its surface has been ground as smooth as possible with a carborundum stone and primed with epoxy.

Fiberglass: Quick and Slick

Fiberglass brings to yacht building what Henry Ford contributed to the manufacture of autos: the speed and efficiency of mass production. No other substance converts so quickly from raw material into floatable hull. Whereas a team of skilled carpenters needs about five and a half months to put together a 40-foot wooden sailboat, a fiberglass 40-footer normally rolls off the line in just 16 days.

The factory shown on these pages, one of the nation's biggest builders of pleasure craft, turns out small glass powerboats at a rate of one every 5.6 minutes. Each hull is shaped inside a reusable concave mold, itself made of fiberglass. In making the hull, a workman first rubs the interior of the mold with wax. Then he sprays on a thin veneer of pigment mixed with polyester resin—a hard-setting liquid plastic. This so-called gel coat becomes the hull's outer surface, providing its color and a porcelain-smooth finish. Then sheets of fiberglass resembling heavy cloth are laid into the mold, one on top of another, and each layer is glued in with more resin. When the hull dries, these laminations form a tough, seamless, waterproof shell that pound for pound has a higher tensile strength than steel.

After the hull is lifted from the mold, workmen complete the interior. Then the fiberglass deck, which has been molded separately *(page 84)*, is fitted on—and another glass boat is ready for launching.

Spraying on what will be the hull's outer skin, a workman covers the inside of a concave mold with a film of tinted polyester resin that is only 17/1,000 of an inch in thickness.

Two kinds of fiberglass material, shown at left in their storage bins, make up the laminations in a typical hull. The bulkier of the two, a fabric of coarsely woven, untwisted strands called roving, alternates with layers of mat, a thinner material made of unwoven fibers pressed together like felt.

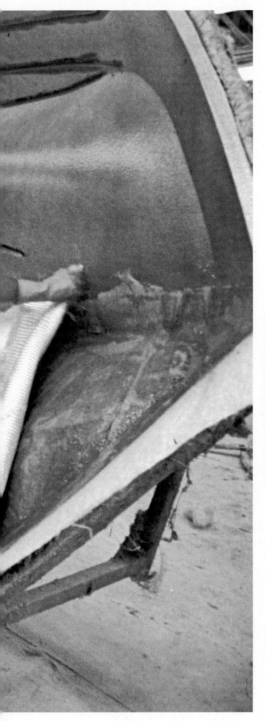

In a process called laying up, workmen apply a lamination of precut fiberglass roving to the inside of an embryo hull that has already received several layers of fiberglass mat. Roving provides most of the hull's strength; the layers of mat add bulk and rigidity.

Between each lamination an adhesive of polyester resin is either sprayed on, as here, or applied with a brush. The resin then is worked carefully into the fiberglass with a squeegee to eliminate possible air pockets.

After curing at room temperature for half an hour, the finished hull lifts easily from its mold. The mold will be cleaned and rewaxed and used to build another hull.

Two factory hands start to build a fiberglass deck by saturating pieces of roving with a binder of polyester resin. The next step will be to lay up the resin-soaked roving in a mold that will give the deck its shape.

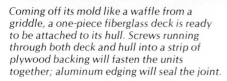

Coming off its mold like a waffle from a griddle, a one-piece fiberglass deck is ready to be attached to its hull. Screws running through both deck and hull into a strip of plywood backing will fasten the units together; aluminum edging will seal the joint.

Workmen spruce up an open cockpit with quilted side panels and wall-to-wall carpeting. The efficiency of assembly-line production permits such touches of luxury at comparatively low cost to the consumer.

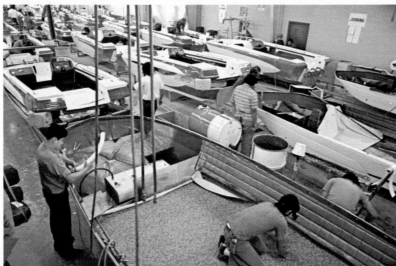

Ranks of fiberglass runabouts stand ready for shipment from the plant. This particular model, a lively 17-footer with a planing hull, takes about 16 working hours to complete, from gel coat to final retouching and buffing.

Aluminum: Light and Tough

Ever since the pioneer ironclads *Merrimac* and *Monitor* battled off the Virginia coast in the most famous naval skirmish of the Civil War, marine architects have been designing boats of metal. Over the ensuing years hulls have been fashioned from wrought iron, rolled steel and copper alloy. But the newest and brightest boatbuilders' metal is aluminum.

No other substance delivers quite the same combination of lightness, sturdiness and structural versatility. Aluminum can be sawed like wood, welded like steel, bent, rolled and extruded into any shape the designer wishes. It neither rusts nor rots. And though, like most metals, aluminum is vulnerable to corrosion, the latest alloys are so resistant they can survive almost indefinitely, even in salt water.

With all these advantages it is not surprising that more and more yachtsmen are ordering up aluminum boats, both stock-built production models and the most elaborate and expensive custom-built racing craft. For example, all three contenders built for the 1974 competition for the America's Cup, yachting's most sought-after prize, were made of aluminum. One of them, *Mariner,* is shown here under construction in Mamaroneck, New York.

Many of the techniques for creating an aluminum boat are quite similar to those of wood construction. In both cases a stress-bearing framework supports a watertight skin. Like a wooden vessel, an aluminum boat has a separately crafted stem that fastens to its keel, and usually it also has longitudinal stringers.

Instead of planks, however, aluminum hulls are sheathed with plates that have been cut to a precise size and rolled to the proper conformation in a special machine. Rather than being screwed or riveted, most aluminum hulls are welded. And while welding can be a relatively fast operation, it is also a complex one.

When aluminum is welded, it shrinks in ways that may pull the whole boat out of shape. Thus, in assembling the framework, the entire structure must first be tack-welded—temporarily secured at various spots—to obtain the correct overall shape. Then the welders go over the framework again to make the junctures permanent. The hull plates, too, are welded with the same two-step process.

After being finished off with several coats of paint, an aluminum hull is hard to distinguish from one made of any other material. For that reason an owner sometimes leaves his boat unpainted to show off its silvery sheen.

The aluminum skeleton of a 12-meter racing yacht stands embraced in a framework of struts that temporarily holds together the hull's main structural members—stem, keel and frames. These elements are almost ready for the welder's torch to bind them securely in place.

Three carefully shaped bow frames lie on a loft floor ready to be fitted into the hull assembly. The flat scoops at the top of the two U-shaped frames are designed to accommodate a groove in the foredeck where a spinnaker pole will be stored.

Cocooned in a mold of steel and concrete, the 12-meter's lead ballast keel cools upside down after pouring. In a few days, it will be broken from the mold and bolted to the hull, with a thin coat of special insulating compound between to prevent corrosion.

Using no other equipment than a hammer and his own highly trained eye, a shipwright exploits aluminum's extreme malleability by pounding a curve into an unheated flange. The flange will be welded to the curved frame in the foreground to strengthen it.

A workman welding together a hatch coaming is enveloped in a cloud of incandescent aluminum-oxide fumes generated by the heat of his torch. The metal clamps bind the coaming to a wooden framework to prevent the heat from distorting the aluminum.

A team of workmen covers the 12-meter's finished skeleton with aluminum plates. An arrangement of clamps and wooden struts holds the plates temporarily in place until they can be first tack-welded and then welded for good. As in all aluminum boats, the shape and thickness of each plate have been carefully gauged by the designer to give needed strength while saving weight where possible.

Fully plated and partially sanded, the hull of the 12-meter reveals its final shape. The joints where the plates are fastened to one another are still visible at this stage, but the whole surface of the hull will be ground down to a uniform finish before it is painted.

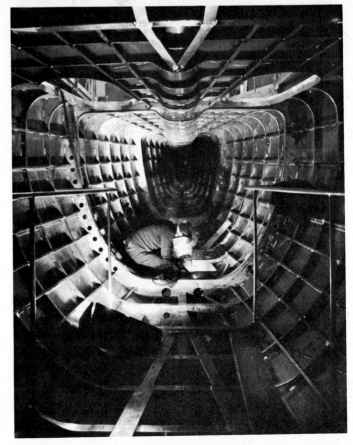

A workman applies some final welds to the hull plates in the narrowing forward section of the 12-meter's interior. Some of the vessel's frames, like the web frame near the workman, have had holes bored in them to cut down their weight. The longitudinals are close together here to counteract "tincanning," a tendency of the aluminum plates to flex inward when they are buffeted by waves.

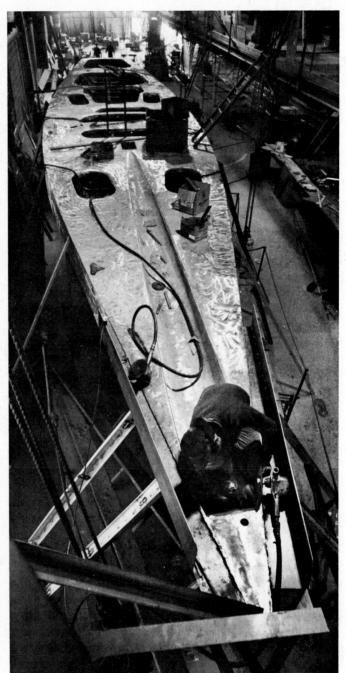

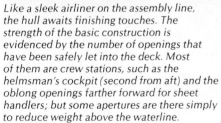

Like a sleek airliner on the assembly line, the hull awaits finishing touches. The strength of the basic construction is evidenced by the number of openings that have been safely let into the deck. Most of them are crew stations, such as the helmsman's cockpit (second from aft) and the oblong openings farther forward for sheet handlers; but some apertures are there simply to reduce weight above the waterline.

A workman, perched on the boat's scaffolded bow in the groove designed to house the spinnaker pole, pauses in his job of sanding the hull's skin with a disk grinder. The process not only levels the welded joints but also roughens the aluminum for the first coat of paint, which would not otherwise adhere to the metal. When the protective coats of paint are applied, any remaining uneven places in the plating will be faired with filler.

4 Every boat needs a power system to make it move. In a rowboat that system is basic: a set of muscles applied to a pair of oars. The modern motorboat derives its power through the expansion of gases from burning fuel in an internal combustion engine. A sailboat converts the wind's power by means of a sail.

Of the three, the most subtle—and perhaps the least understood—is the interaction between wind and sail. At its simplest level, the push of the breeze against a sail held at right angles to it is comprehensible to anybody who has ever tried to fold a beach blanket in a fresh breeze or attempted to stand against a gale. The wind simply pushes everything along in its

THE PUSH OR PULL TO MAKE IT GO

path. But a sail has an additional and much more sophisticated way of working. It not only acts to push the boat along with the wind, it also can pull a boat almost straight toward the source of the wind.

This marvelous capacity is strikingly demonstrated by the lean 12-meter-class yacht on the opposite page. Close-hauled on the starboard tack—that is, with its sails trimmed in and the wind coming over the right side of its bow—this sloop is plunging ahead as directly into the wind's eye as virtually any sailboat can go. (If a boat were headed directly into the wind, its sails would flap, or luff, like a flag in the breeze, and the craft would stop.)

The secret of the sails' upwind pulling power lies in their shape and in the angle at which they meet the moving airstream. When filled by wind, a sail takes on a curve that resembles the arced cross section of an airplane wing. And as with a wing, aerodynamic forces develop along its two sides; these forces do the real work. In a wing they provide the lift that keeps the airplane aloft. In a sail they generate power that, when transmitted to the hull through spars and rigging, literally sucks the boat to windward. This complex but fascinating force—paradoxically called thrust—is explained in detail overleaf.

Yacht designers and sailmakers search constantly for the best ways to apply this principle to the many kinds and combinations of sails carried by modern yachts. They have found, for example, that a sail with a long leading edge is the most efficient for going upwind. Consequently, sails on racing craft have become taller and narrower, while the masts and rigging that hold them up have become lighter and stronger.

For all its efficiency, a sailboat's rig tends to be elaborate and extensive; and its fuel—the wind—is notoriously undependable. By contrast, a powerboat's internal combustion engines are marvels of compact dependability. They were not always so. The steam engines that changed maritime history at the end of the 18th Century were great clanking contraptions that needed almost as much attention as the sails they replaced.

The first seagoing internal combustion engines, developed nearly 100 years later, were primitive gasoline burners that delivered only a few horsepower. Today, most inboard power plants are powerful automobile engines, modified for a marine habitat. The outboard, however, is a true marine creation, developed in 1906 by Cameron Waterman, a Detroit lawyer, to be clamped on a skiff's transom. Comparatively lightweight and highly maneuverable, the outboard has contributed more to the growth of pleasure boating than has any other factor.

On both inboards and outboards, the engine moves the boat by spinning a propeller. Its blades bite into the water and throw a stream to the rear—just as a fan blows a draft of air. As the water thus pushed meets the resistance of the water beyond it, the boat is moved forward. This thrust is much more direct than the aerodynamic forces at work on a sail. But, push or pull, the same effect is generated: an impetus that makes the boat go.

Under gracefully curved canvas that can extract the energy from moving air—even when it is coming from almost straight ahead—a 12-meter racing yacht drives into the wind.

As a boat's bow points toward the oncoming wind, here blowing from the top of the illustration, the sail splits the airstream. As long as the boat does not turn directly to windward, its sail can exploit this dislocation of air currents, using the wind's energy to move the vessel ahead (heavy arrow).

The plus and minus signs in the diagram below reflect variations in pressure that occur when wind flows across a sail. Lower pressures on its outside curve result from the greater distance that the leeward wind stream must travel. Just behind the mast, turbulence neutralizes the pressure difference.

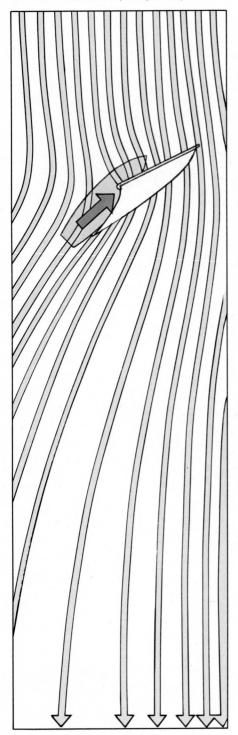

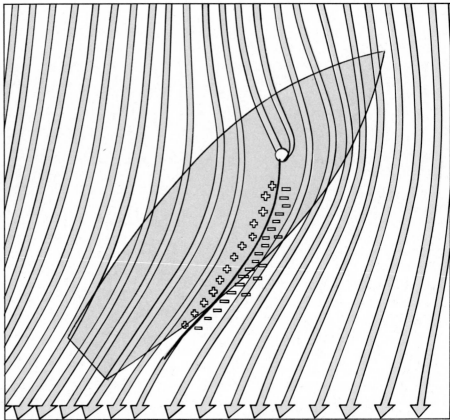

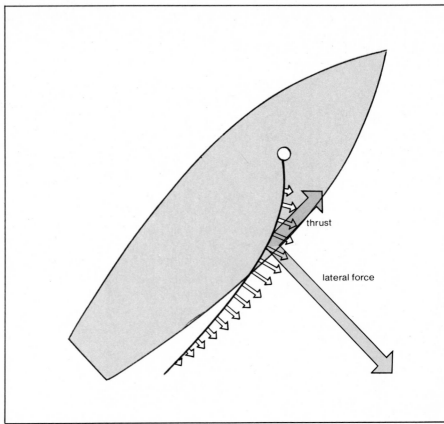

The small arrows springing from the sail's leeward side (right) represent the forces generated by wind—the pressure imbalance between the sail's two sides. The combined effect is demonstrated by the large arrows: a substantial lateral, or sideways, force and a much smaller, but vital, forward thrust.

The Sail as an Airfoil

The apparently baffling forces that propel a sailboat toward the wind are actually quite predictable. They go to work when a suitably shaped airfoil, i.e., a sail, is placed in the wind's path.

A sail divides the wind moving past it into twin currents of air. These currents flow at unequal velocities. The reason is simple: because of the sail's shape and its angle—or attitude—relative to the wind's source, the currents have different distances to travel. While the air molecules on the upwind side do not significantly change their speed, those in the outer airstream that have to go around the bulge of the sail's leeward side must move faster in order to arrive at the sail's trailing edge at the same time.

As the airstream to leeward picks up speed, a physical law first described by the Swiss physicist Daniel Bernoulli in 1738 takes effect. Bernoulli's law dictates that when a stream of either air or water accelerates, it exerts less pressure on the surfaces it flows past. Thus the air pressure drops on the sail's leeward side in comparison with the pressure on its windward side. This difference in pressure is what moves the sailboat into the wind. Although the difference works primarily—along with the wind pressure—to push the boat sideways (bottom, left) or to heel it over, it also imparts a firm forward thrust.

Actually, no combination of sail is a perfect aerodynamic mechanism. To begin with, few sails are ideal airfoils, especially when rigged on a mast. The mast disturbs air currents, which flow turbulently around it and inhibit the pressure differential that creates the aerodynamic power in the sail's bulge. Wind that hits the mast head on thus dissipates its useful force (diagram, top left).

Also, since the strongest aerodynamic force exerted by the wind on the sail shoves it to the side, the boat needs some counteracting device if it is to make use of the remaining forward pull. Such an aid is built into the underwater shape of the hull: a keel or a centerboard with a thin, streamlined shape that cuts forward easily but moves sideways with reluctance.

Finally, a boat underway reacts quickly to the friction of water on the hull—the force known as drag. The vessel's acceleration soon levels off as drag increases with velocity; eventually the drag neutralizes any further gain in speed. When a boat attains this point of equilibrium (right), it sails smoothly ahead until a shift of the wind's direction or a change in its velocity upsets the balance.

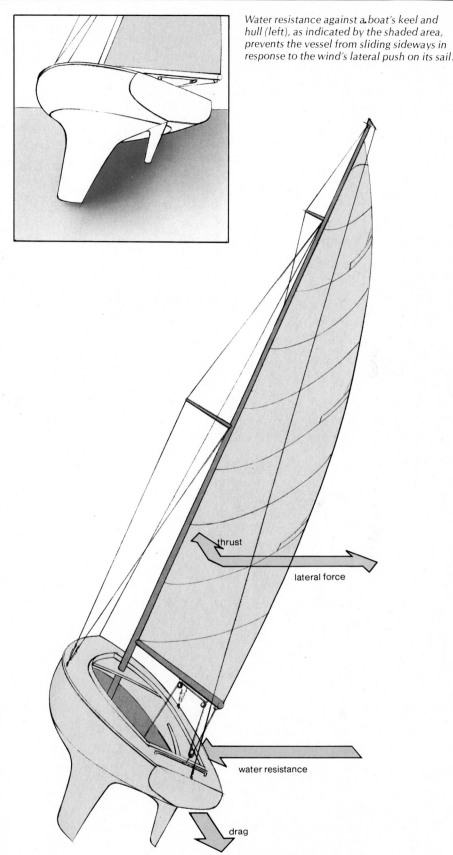

Water resistance against a boat's keel and hull (left), as indicated by the shaded area, prevents the vessel from sliding sideways in response to the wind's lateral push on its sail.

The boat above is moving forward at a steady rate, dynamically balanced between conflicting forces of wind and water. Water resistance counters the wind force's sideways push, which heels the boat to leeward. The water's drag, caused by forward movement, prevents further acceleration. Only if the wind blows harder will the speed increase.

Sails for All Headings

A boat's basic airfoil, explained on the preceding pages, is the mainsail, which can propel a boat in any direction—except, of course, right into the wind's eye. But for all its aerodynamic pulling power, the mainsail does even better when it is teamed up with a jib, a triangular headsail set in front of the mast.

A jib not only increases sail area, it also multiplies efficiency by channeling and smoothing out the airflow past the mainsail (diagrams, right). In the process, the headsail reduces the area of turbulence on the mainsail just behind the mast; and the jib itself, attached to a thin wire stay, suffers very little from turbulence.

Headsails come in various cuts and sizes (page 102), designed for different wind strengths and directions. The small working jib (second from left) is a utility sail that can be carried going either into the wind or with the wind across the side. The larger genoa (third from left), a sail that overlaps the mast, delivers even more pulling power on either of these headings. Sailing before the wind, nothing speeds a boat along faster than a spinnaker (far right). Now the mainsail is at right angles to the wind and acts not as an airfoil, but simply as a surface for the wind to shove against. The spinnaker, however, provides not only added sail area but some aerodynamic pull as well.

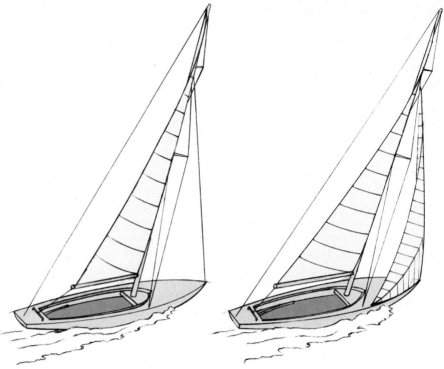

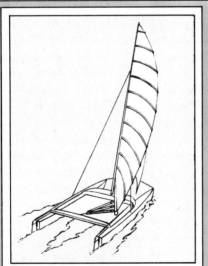

Shaping Up a Sail

No sail can hold a perfect airfoil curve, under every condition, because of the cloth's flexibility. One way to give a sail better shape is to stiffen it with battens —wood or plastic strips—that stabilize the trailing edge of the mainsail or jib. Used full length, as on this speedy catamaran, they hold the entire mainsail in a proper aerodynamic curve.

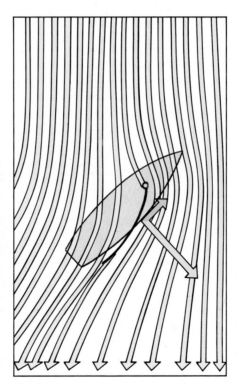

The least efficient way of sailing is usually going to windward under mainsail alone. The sail generates both lateral and forward aerodynamic force, but the wind sweeping over the bow is barely used, and the airstream down the sail's lee side breaks away, wasting power. Also, mast turbulence is high.

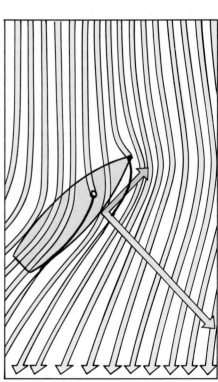

More speed and control result when a working jib augments the main. The jib uses wind coming over the bow and channels the airstream along the mainsail's lee side, adding thrust and cutting mast turbulence. The result (arrows) is more lateral force, but also a proportionate increase in thrust.

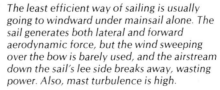

thrust

heeling force

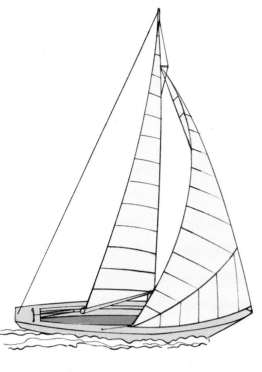

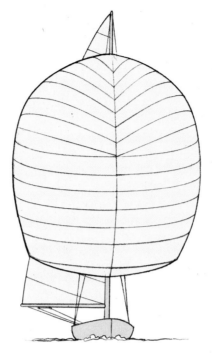

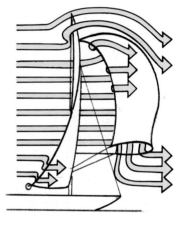

In this profile view of a spinnaker at work the wind arrows show that while most air currents shove against the sail, some stream out over the top in a flow that creates aerodynamic lift and helps keep the sail full.

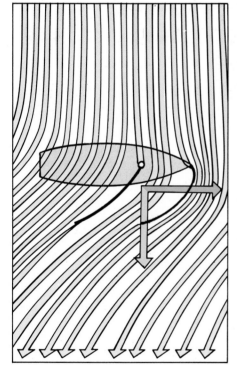

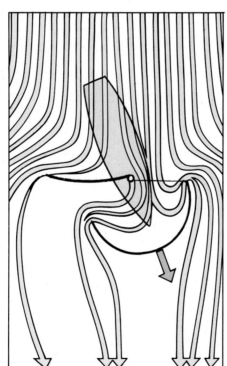

Faster sailing comes on a reach, with the wind blowing on the beam; this is especially true if the working jib is replaced by an overlapping genoa. On a reach, sails are let out, easing the lateral force that causes the boat to heel (pink arrow) and using more of the wind's energy to thrust the boat ahead.

A boat carries the most sail area when running before the wind, using a parachute spinnaker. Here most of the boat's forward movement comes simply from the wind pushing against the sails; nevertheless, the huge spinnaker adds considerable speed and some aerodynamic thrust (above, right).

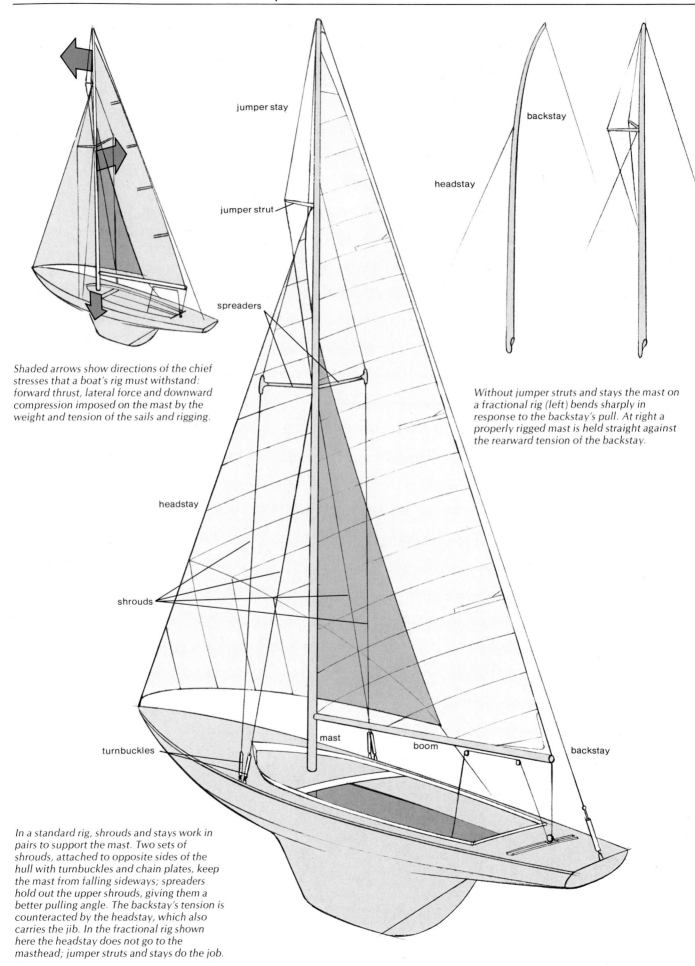

jumper stay

jumper strut

spreaders

headstay

shrouds

turnbuckles

mast

boom

backstay

backstay

headstay

Shaded arrows show directions of the chief stresses that a boat's rig must withstand: forward thrust, lateral force and downward compression imposed on the mast by the weight and tension of the sails and rigging.

Without jumper struts and stays the mast on a fractional rig (left) bends sharply in response to the backstay's pull. At right a properly rigged mast is held straight against the rearward tension of the backstay.

In a standard rig, shrouds and stays work in pairs to support the mast. Two sets of shrouds, attached to opposite sides of the hull with turnbuckles and chain plates, keep the mast from falling sideways; spreaders hold out the upper shrouds, giving them a better pulling angle. The backstay's tension is counteracted by the headstay, which also carries the jib. In the fractional rig shown here the headstay does not go to the masthead; jumper struts and stays do the job.

A Rig to Carry the Load

At rest, a sail is no more than a swatch of cloth. To be effective, it needs a rig—a mast, or spar, to hold it up and a web of ropes and wires to transmit to the boat the tremendous energy the sail extracts from the wind. A vessel's rig is thus the equivalent of an engine's drive shaft, a means for converting power into useful motion.

The rig's main elements are its spars and its standing rigging, which includes all the stationary wires that hold the mast in place. In support of these components is the running rigging, comprising the lines that control the sails: the halyards, used to hoist and lower the sails; and the sheets, usually Dacron rope, that pull the sails in and let them out.

The chief spars are the mast, to which the forward edge of the mainsail is fastened, and the boom. A horizontal spar attached to the mast, the boom holds the sail's foot, or bottom edge, and pivots on the mast so that the sail can be trimmed on either side of the boat.

Standing rigging, usually either wires or thin steel rods, is carefully positioned to balance the sails' pressures. Leading from high on the mast to the bow and stern are two wires—the headstay and backstay—that withstand the force of the sails' thrust. On some boats the headstay is attached to the mast below the top—an arrangement called a fractional rig *(left)*, designed for a relatively small, easily handled jib. In a masthead rig *(right)* the headstay goes all the way to the top of the mast, allowing for a larger jib and thus more power. The side rigging wires, which counteract the sails' heeling force, are shrouds. Strong metal flanges, known as chain plates, connect the shrouds and stays to the hull, and the wires' tension can be fine-tuned by means of turnbuckles *(right, bottom)*.

Essential though it is, a boat's rig has certain drawbacks; it creates wind resistance that slows a boat's progress and adds weight aloft that impairs stability. Thus solid wood masts have long since given way to hollow wood or metal spars, tapered at the top to cut down weight. The need for light, strong material becomes ever more pressing as the masts of modern racing yachts rise higher and their sails grow taller and more efficient. It is estimated that the slender 80-foot mast of a 12-meter sloop carrying a mainsail and genoa in a fresh breeze is subjected to a compression force of 36 tons. A failure of any vital part of the rig would instantly turn the whole intricate arrangement into a useless, chaotic tangle.

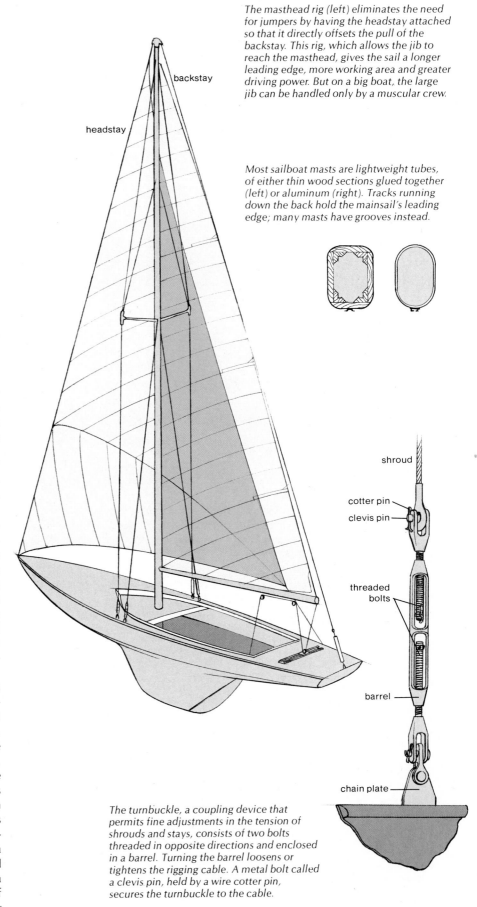

The masthead rig (left) eliminates the need for jumpers by having the headstay attached so that it directly offsets the pull of the backstay. This rig, which allows the jib to reach the masthead, gives the sail a longer leading edge, more working area and greater driving power. But on a big boat, the large jib can be handled only by a muscular crew.

Most sailboat masts are lightweight tubes, of either thin wood sections glued together (left) or aluminum (right). Tracks running down the back hold the mainsail's leading edge; many masts have grooves instead.

backstay

headstay

shroud

cotter pin

clevis pin

threaded bolts

barrel

chain plate

The turnbuckle, a coupling device that permits fine adjustments in the tension of shrouds and stays, consists of two bolts threaded in opposite directions and enclosed in a barrel. Turning the barrel loosens or tightens the rigging cable. A metal bolt called a clevis pin, held by a wire cotter pin, secures the turnbuckle to the cable.

The Basic Rigs

A tall triangle held aloft by a spar: this, after almost 2,000 years, is still the basic geometry of the efficient fore-and-aft sail plan that, in a variety of guises, powers almost all sailing craft today. Even when a yacht carries a number of sails on more than one mast, the canvas on each mast is usually arranged in the same compact triangle, echoing the earliest fore-and-aft rig, the lateen shown below.

Modern sailing craft use six basic sail plans. Most of them, as shown here, are built around a lofty triangular mainsail, in a configuration called the Marconi rig. (The name was suggested by the towering masts put up for Guglielmo Marconi's wireless radio just before the triangular main came into use.) Some traditional craft, such as the catboat and schooner, still use a gaff rig, in which a shorter, four-sided sail hangs from a spar called a gaff.

The most popular modern rig is the sloop, whose one mast supports a mainsail and a jib; its close relative, the cutter, is also single-masted. Many boats, however, carry a split rig in which the sail area is partitioned into several elements and set on two masts. Dividing the sail area usually reduces its aerodynamic efficiency, but a number of smaller sails are easier to handle than one or two huge ones. While all the rigs except the cat can carry many combinations of jibs, staysails and spinnakers (page 102), the boat that piles on more sails than any other is the schooner, a traditional rig that, to many seamen, is still the prettiest afloat.

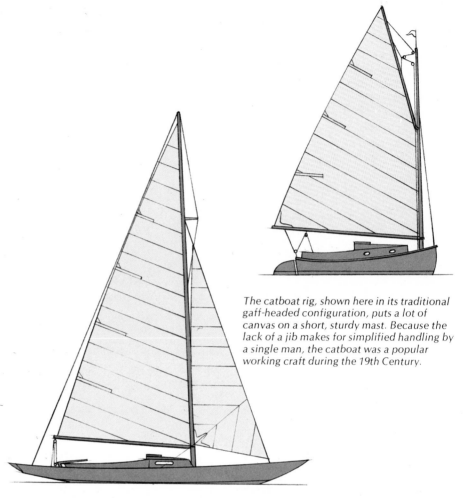

The catboat rig, shown here in its traditional gaff-headed configuration, puts a lot of canvas on a short, sturdy mast. Because the lack of a jib makes for simplified handling by a single man, the catboat was a popular working craft during the 19th Century.

Three-cornered Ancestor

Ancestor of all fore-and-aft sails, this simple but effective lateen rig is an Arab invention that dates back to the time of Christ. The lateen sail is still seen on Nile barges and Arab dhows; it is also carried by thousands of small board boats that sail on U.S. waters today.

Moving the mast slightly aft and adding a jib turns a catboat into a sloop. With a taller, more efficient Marconi mainsail and room for a choice of headsails—jib, genoa, spinnaker—sloops are fast and responsive. Most racing sailboats carry this rig.

A cutter carries its mast farther aft than does a sloop, leaving space for several headsails to be set at once—in this case a jib, the forwardmost sail set on the headstay running from the masthead to the bowsprit, and an inner headsail, called a forestaysail.

The yawl, its tall mainmast supplemented by a short mizzenmast stepped behind helm and rudder, is the most popular two-masted rig. The mainsail and jib do most of the work, while the little mizzen, easily raised and lowered, helps balance and steer the boat.

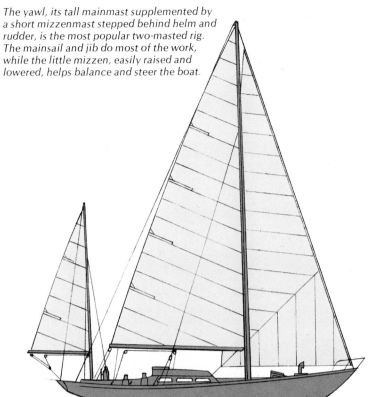

In the ketch rig the mizzenmast is taller than on a yawl and is set forward of the rudder and, usually, the helm. With its evenly divided sail area, the ketch makes an excellent cruising rig, with a comfortable balance between headsails and mizzen.

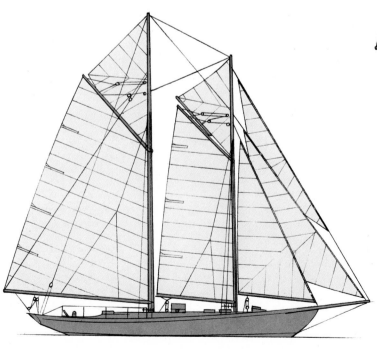

On a schooner the shorter mast, the foremast, is ahead of the mainmast. This gaff-rigged schooner carries a mainsail and foresail, each surmounted by a topsail, and, ahead of the foremast, a forestaysail on a boom, a working jib and flying jib set from the bowsprit.

Headsails

The working jib (left) has a short foot, or bottom, that does not overlap the mast and often has a boom for easier control. The double-headsail rig (right) combines a forestaysail with a jib for extra pulling power.

Genoa jibs for sailing to windward come in varying sizes for different wind strengths; they are efficient but difficult to handle. The reacher (right) is a high-cut genoa—less likely to trail in the water when the boat heels.

Staysails

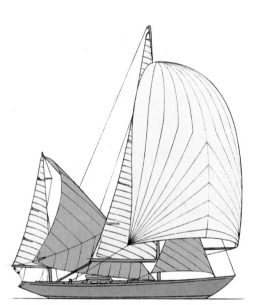
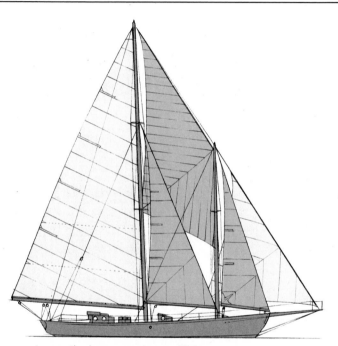

With the wind abeam, this yawl lifts a panoply of canvas that includes, besides main and mizzen, a mizzen staysail hoisted on the mizzenmast, a reaching spinnaker and a small spinnaker staysail that sets below it.

A staysail schooner carries an efficient triangular main staysail between the masts instead of the old-fashioned foresail; above it is a four-sided fisherman's staysail. A forestaysail and jib complete the plan.

Storm Sails

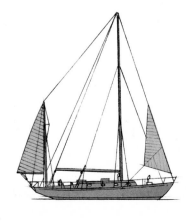

Small sails, made of strong fabrics heavily reinforced to withstand high winds, steady a boat and keep it under control in a blow. The sloop at left carries a storm, or spitfire, jib on the headstay and a storm trysail on the mast. The yawl rides under a storm jib and mizzen without a mainsail—a combination frequently referred to as jib and jigger.

The Search for Speed

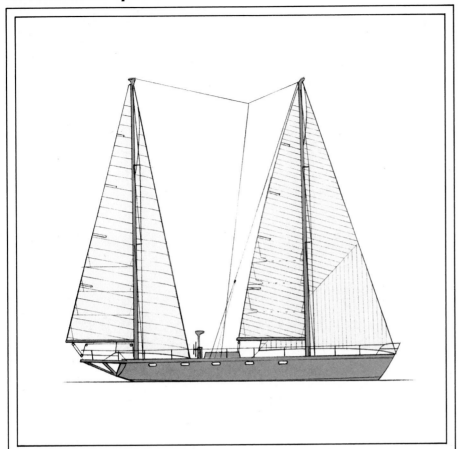

On the 79-foot ocean-racing yacht Ondine, the conventional ketch rig has been radically modified to make the most efficient use of a two-masted sail plan. The masts are the same height, and they are widely separated so that each can carry the complementary sets of sails shown here: mainsail and genoa jib on the mainmast; mizzen and mizzen staysail on the aftermast. The rig, essentially two sloops on one hull, sped the vessel to a course record for the Newport-Bermuda race in 1974: 635 miles in just over 68 hours.

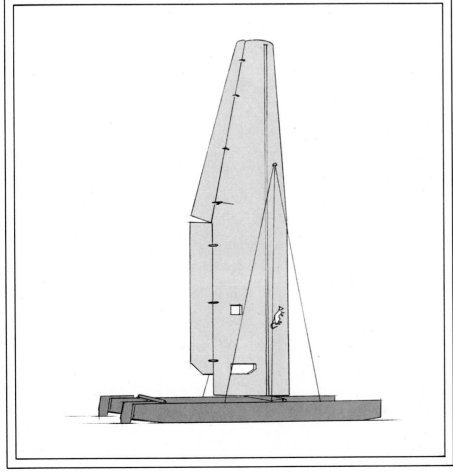

The ultimate catboat, Miss Nylex of Australia, a world-champion C-class catamaran, makes the best use of aerodynamic forces in its single, rigid sail—basically an upended airplane wing. Made of fabric stretched on a wood frame, the sail presents to the wind a better-shaped airfoil than a soft sail; and because mast and sail are one piece, no mast turbulence disrupts wind flow. Unlike the highly specialized proa Crossbow (page 57), Miss Nylex is just as maneuverable as any catamaran, yet can sail nearly 30 mph.

A Seagoing Power Plant

The sail is quiet and graceful, and the outboard compact and versatile (pages 110-111). But the most powerful and efficient device for pushing pleasure boats around is the inboard engine. Like most internal combustion engines, it burns fuel to move pistons back and forth and impart rotary motion to a drive shaft. In this, the inboard is indistinguishable from the power plant under the hood of almost any truck or car; indeed, most boat inboards are at heart automotive engines. But the marine environment poses distinctive problems that require modifications. These are emphasized in the drawing at right.

The most significant adaptations concern the cooling system. Inboards, like all internal combustion engines, generate a lot of heat. In a water-cooled automotive engine, heat is absorbed by fresh water, which is cooled in turn by air blowing across the radiator. In inboard pleasure boats, the power plants are enclosed in an engine compartment, so that air cooling is not practicable. Marine engines thus need another system for keeping cool.

One obvious answer is to scoop up a bit of the water that surrounds the boat, swirl it through the engine and pump it back out again—and many systems do exactly that, particularly if the boat operates only in fresh water. But for boats that go into the ocean another method is desirable. Since salt precipitates out of seawater when it is heated to more than 150°— below the temperature at which engines work best—passages in any engine cooled directly by seawater tend to become caked and corroded. Therefore a fresh-water cooling system is used (shown in green), in which fresh water is cooled not by air but by seawater (blue). The heart of this system is a heat exchanger—the marine counterpart to a car radiator. Seawater pumped into the heat exchanger (far right) extracts heat from the fresh-water coolant and then goes overboard through the exhaust. A similar heat exchanger cools the lubricating oil.

The lack of a fast-flowing airstream poses another problem for the enclosed inboard: fuel fumes can collect and be ignited by a stray spark from the engine. As protection from this hazard, the Coast Guard requires a flame arrester to be fitted on every marine inboard (above). And marine alternators, which charge the batteries, are built with protective shields.

With these adaptations, the inboard engine, securely mounted to keep its place even in the roughest going, is a dependable, seaworthy power plant.

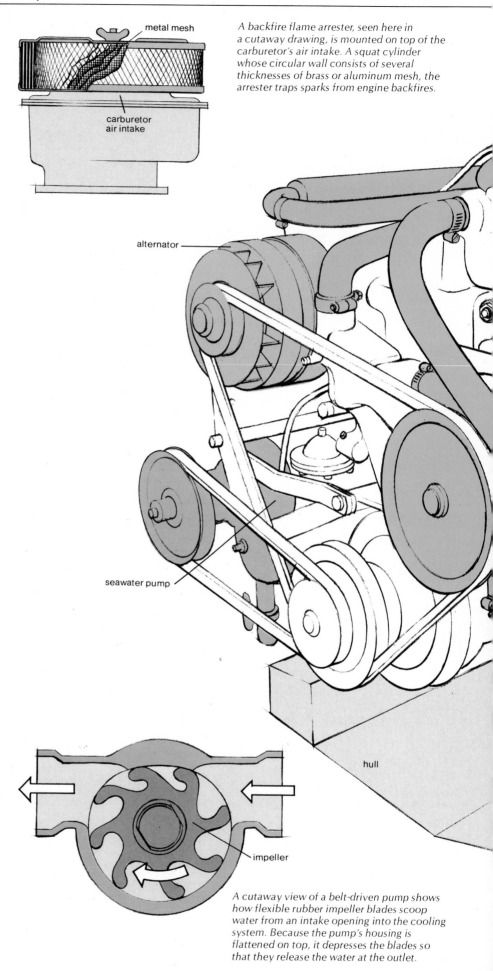

A backfire flame arrester, seen here in a cutaway drawing, is mounted on top of the carburetor's air intake. A squat cylinder whose circular wall consists of several thicknesses of brass or aluminum mesh, the arrester traps sparks from engine backfires.

A cutaway view of a belt-driven pump shows how flexible rubber impeller blades scoop water from an intake opening into the cooling system. Because the pump's housing is flattened on top, it depresses the blades so that they release the water at the outlet.

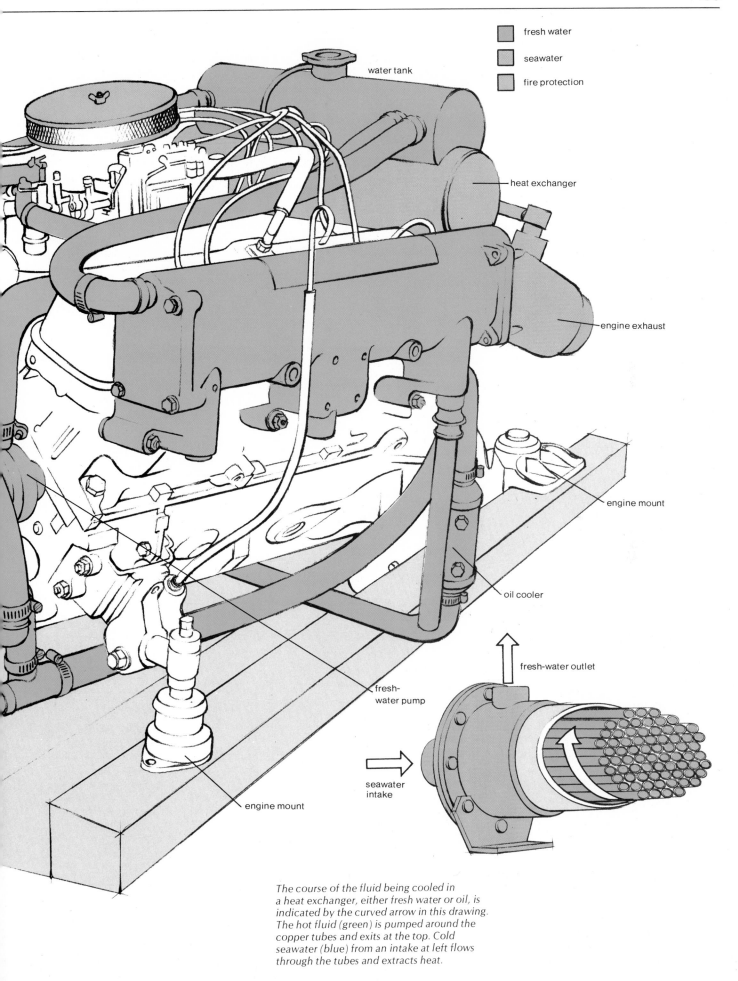

fresh water

seawater

fire protection

water tank

heat exchanger

engine exhaust

engine mount

oil cooler

fresh-water outlet

fresh-water pump

seawater intake

engine mount

The course of the fluid being cooled in a heat exchanger, either fresh water or oil, is indicated by the curved arrow in this drawing. The hot fluid (green) is pumped around the copper tubes and exits at the top. Cold seawater (blue) from an intake at left flows through the tubes and extracts heat.

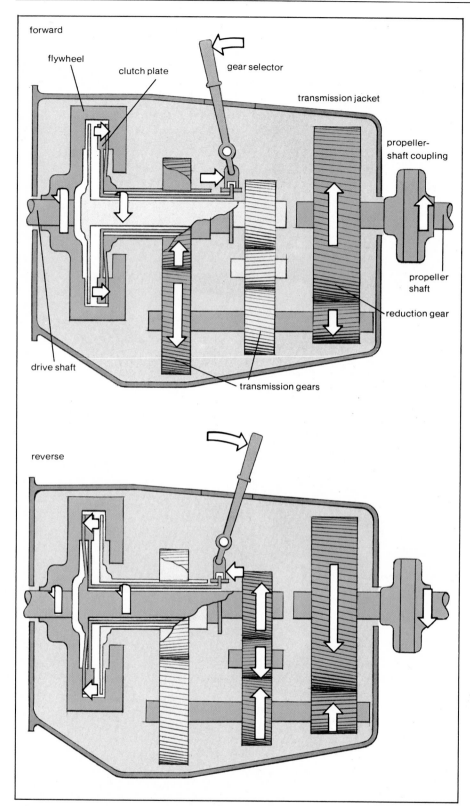

The flow of power through a marine transmission is shown in green in these two drawings. When the gear selector is pushed to the left (top), the forward clutch plates engage the flywheel, attached to the engine's output shaft. This transmits the shaft's rotation to the forward gear combination, so that the large gear at right, connected to the propeller shaft, turns in the same direction as the drive shaft. At bottom in reverse, a second clutch plate directs power through a set of gears that reverse the rotation of the propeller shaft.

Transmission and Drive

Like the motor itself, the system of gears and shafts that transmits a marine engine's power to the propeller must be rugged. Since boats brake by reversal of the propeller's rotation, the engine-to-prop power train must be able to withstand the shock of being slammed directly from forward into reverse.

A boat's transmission is much simpler than an automobile's. Since no ascending sequence of gears is required to bring the boat to cruising speed, only one gear ratio in either forward or reverse is needed. But because engines run best at a higher level of rpm's than do marine propellers, many boat transmissions have reduction gears to slow the propeller's rotation.

A marine transmission, like the one shown in the schematic drawings at left, consists of a set of forward and reverse gears that, when engaged by a clutch, convey the engine's power to the propeller shaft. The reduction gears, at the rear end of the transmission, include a small gear meshed with a larger one that turns the propeller shaft; every turn of the smaller gear rotates the larger one a fraction of one revolution. Thus, in a 2-to-1 reduction-gear system, two turns of the smaller gear produce only a single turn of the larger gear—and of the propeller.

On an inboard boat the simplest way of getting power from engine to propeller (opposite) is by direct drive, a straight shaft from transmission to propeller. Another system, called V drive, allows the engine to be placed in the boat's stern, providing more cabin or cockpit space. A specialized alternative is jet drive, which eliminates both external propeller and rudder, an advantage for boats operating in shoal waters, where a prop might snag.

Gasoline versus Diesel

Gasoline engines cost less than diesels, provide more horsepower per pound of weight and accelerate faster. But diesels are generally more reliable, use cheaper fuel and are much safer than gasoline engines, whose volatile fuel is a serious fire hazard. Since the diesel's fuel is injected into the cylinder under high pressure and ignites without any need for a spark plug, the engine requires no ignition system—a system that in a marine gasoline engine is vulnerable to corrosion and short circuits. Conversely, the diesel's high-pressure combustion requires a hefty engine block, making it impractical for many small boats.

direct drive

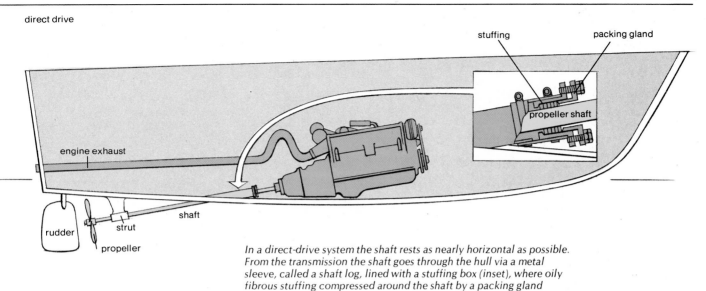

stuffing

packing gland

propeller shaft

engine exhaust

rudder

strut

propeller

shaft

In a direct-drive system the shaft rests as nearly horizontal as possible. From the transmission the shaft goes through the hull via a metal sleeve, called a shaft log, lined with a stuffing box (inset), where oily fibrous stuffing compressed around the shaft by a packing gland prevents water from leaking through the opening in the hull.

V drive

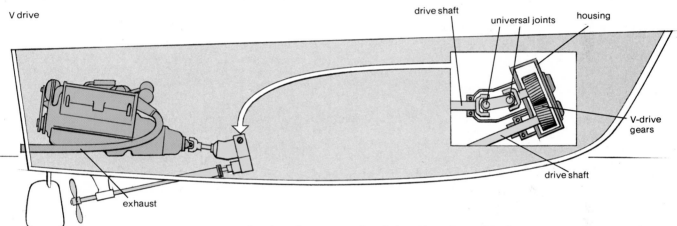

drive shaft

universal joints

housing

V-drive gears

drive shaft

exhaust

With V drive the engine is placed aft and faces forward. In the version shown here the upper drive shaft is connected to the lower by means of a flexible universal joint (inset) and two gears that transmit power to the propeller. In some V-drive systems the gears are beveled, or angled, to eliminate the need for a universal joint.

jet drive

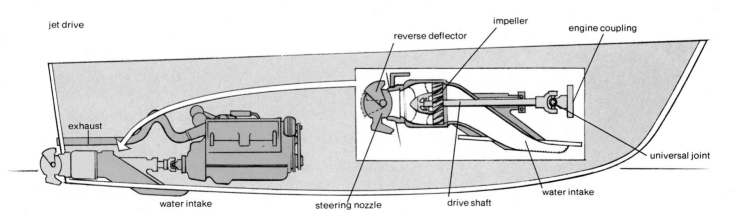

reverse deflector

impeller

engine coupling

exhaust

universal joint

water intake

water intake

steering nozzle

drive shaft

The key components on the jet-drive system are the impeller—an internal propeller that acts like a high-speed water pump—and a swivel-mounted nozzle (inset). Water drawn in and put under pressure by the impeller jets from the nozzle and thrusts the boat forward. For reverse, a deflector plate covers the nozzle and diverts the jet forward.

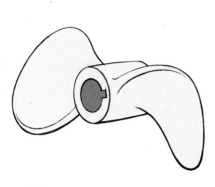

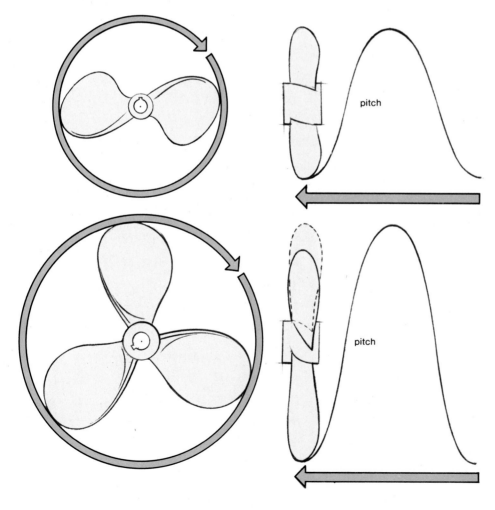

The basic propeller types used are the two-
and three-bladed models illustrated here. The
prop shaft fits into the propeller's bore,
i.e., the hole in the hub. A keyway notched
into the bore embraces a key fitted into the
shaft so that shaft and prop spin together.

These two propellers have turning circles of
different diameters, but their pitch is the
same because a propeller's pitch is a product
of its diameter and the angle of its blades.
Thus the theoretical advance of the small
two-bladed prop, with its sharply angled
blades, is identical to the theoretical advance
of the three-bladed prop (bottom right),
whose diameter is greater but whose blades
are set into the hub at a less sharp angle.

Propellers for Thrust

The key to the driving power ultimately delivered by a marine engine is the propeller, which converts the drive shaft's rotation into propulsive thrust. This occurs as the angled faces of a turning propeller's blades force strong currents backward, producing pressure against the surrounding water that shoves the boat ahead.

The amount of thrust a propeller generates for an engine of any given power rating is related to its diameter, the number of blades, their shape and so-called pitch. A small change in any of these characteristics can mean a significant alteration in thrust. Of these factors, the two most critical are the number of blades and the diameter of their turning circles.

Big powerboats, such as cruisers, which need powerful thrust to move their weight along, generally use three-bladed propellers with relatively big diameters—and broad-faced blades—like the one in the larger drawing at left. Such a propeller provides plenty of thrust, but it also requires a hefty power plant to turn it. Two-bladed props with smaller diameters and slimmer blades (far left) are suited for lighter, high-speed boats, such as outboard racers, with less weight to push.

Pitch (left) is the theoretical distance in inches the tips of the blades travel forward during one revolution. Thus a propeller with 10-inch pitch would ideally move through the water 10 inches with each turn. But water, being a fluid, does not provide firm resistance for the blades to push against, so a propeller with 10-inch pitch may move only seven inches. This difference, called propeller slip, affects every prop, however well designed.

Another phenomenon that can affect propellers is a nautical affliction known as cavitation (at near right). It occurs when the blades churn up the water in such a way that small vapor cavities form around them to create a partial vacuum. With nothing to push against, the blades race around, but produce no thrust.

Cavitation becomes a problem when propeller blades start to turn too fast; in fact, a certain amount of cavitation at the blade tips is normal, as shown in the illustration at right, above. The real difficulty starts whenever the cavities multiply and move down the blades so that there is nothing to push against.

Occasionally cavitation results from a nicked blade. Warm water, less dense than cold water, can also be the culprit. In any case, the only immediate remedy is to slow down the engine, thus letting the prop get a full grip on the water again.

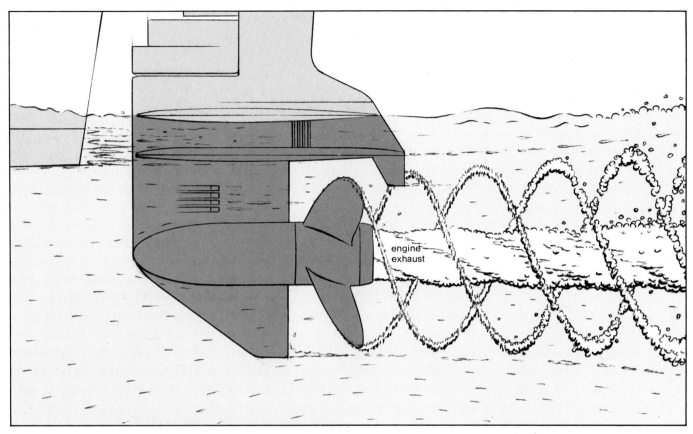

engine exhaust

Hurling the water behind in a spreading, turbulent discharge called a thrust cone, an outboard's propeller drives a boat ahead. The spiraling bubbles coming off the tips are traces of harmless tip cavitation. The stream of exhaust bubbles discharging from the hub does not affect the prop's performance.

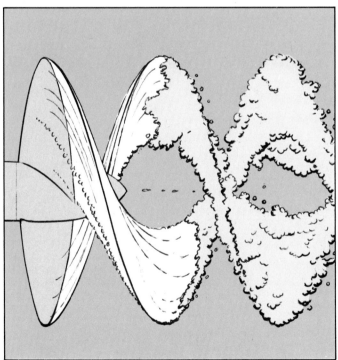

Cavitating badly, the propeller shown above is generating very little thrust. The outer surfaces of the blades are moving so fast that water cannot flow together behind them; instead, vapor-filled cavities create a partial vacuum. Only water flowing over the hub and inner parts of the blades remains intact.

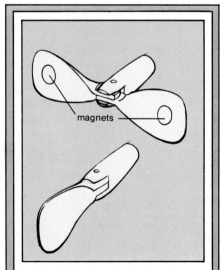

magnets

A Solution for Sailboats

The folding propeller was designed as an answer to the sailboat's need for a propeller that causes the least possible drag when not in use. As the propeller spins, the swiveled blades are forced open by centrifugal force. When the boat is sailing, water flow folds the blades and the magnets keep them closed.

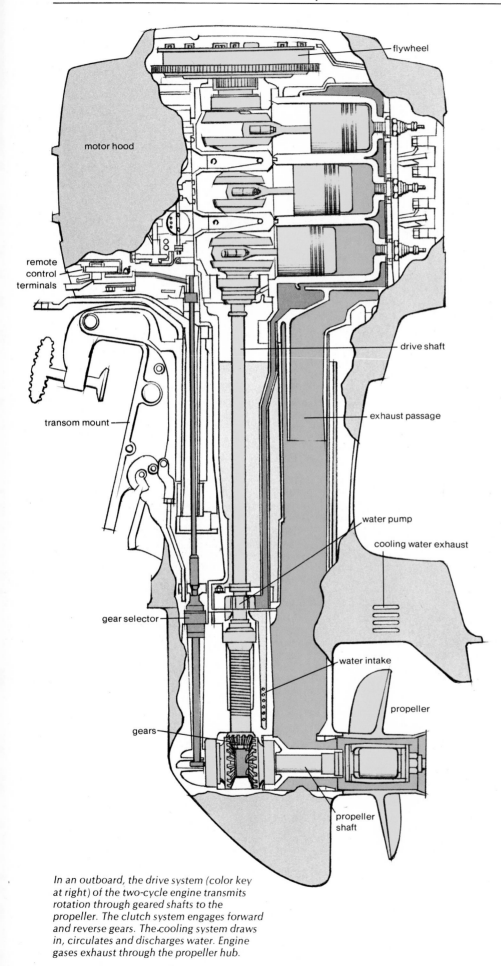

flywheel

motor hood

remote control terminals

transom mount

drive shaft

exhaust passage

water pump

cooling water exhaust

gear selector

water intake

propeller

gears

propeller shaft

In an outboard, the drive system (color key at right) of the two-cycle engine transmits rotation through geared shafts to the propeller. The clutch system engages forward and reverse gears. The cooling system draws in, circulates and discharges water. Engine gases exhaust through the propeller hub.

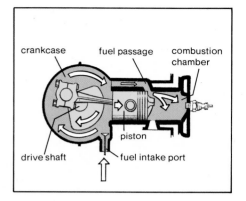

crankcase   fuel passage   combustion chamber

piston

drive shaft   fuel intake port

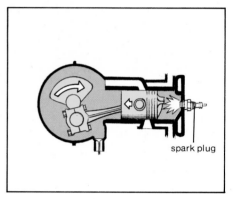

spark plug

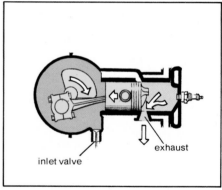

inlet valve   exhaust

The two-cycle engine delivers power with every other piston stroke. As the piston, beginning its compression stroke (top), moves to compress the mixture of unburned fuel and air (purple) in the cylinder, it draws the next charge of fuel and air behind it into the crankcase. After the compressed mixture is ignited by the spark plug (middle), the piston, starting its power stroke, moves past an exhaust valve (bottom), allowing burned gases (pink) to escape. At the end of the stroke, it will force unburned fuel from the crankcase into the cylinder through the inlet valve to set up another compression stroke.

    power train

clutch system

cooling

exhaust

The Compact Outboard

Unlike the inboard engine, which was adapted for marine use from an automotive motor, the outboard was intended from the start just for boats. Basically it is an internal combustion engine stood on end, with its drive shaft vertical, so that the entire assembly can be mounted on a boat's transom. Overall the outboard is designed to be as compact as possible.

Invented at the turn of the century as a small, portable power plant chiefly for rowboats, the outboard now drives every kind and shape of boat up to overnight cruisers. In fact, 8 out of every 10 powerboats, including virtually all those under 15 feet, are made for outboards.

The key to the outboard's success is the saving of weight and boat-space afforded by the compactness of its two-cycle power system (near left). Since every second stroke of the piston in the cylinder generates power—as opposed to every fourth stroke for a four-cycle engine—the two-cycle outboard produces more push per pound of its own weight than does the normal inboard. The drive system, encased in the engine's lower unit, is equally light and compact. A vertical crankshaft transmits power to the short propeller shaft by means of three simple gears (top right)—at the same time energizing a pump that operates the cooling system.

Besides being compact, the outboard engine has other advantages over the inboard. Initially, it is less expensive: a 100 horsepower outboard costs about 50 per cent less than an equivalent inboard system. Since the outboard rides on the transom, it requires no engine compartment, thus freeing more space. It poses little fire hazard since any fuel leakage is likely to be overboard, rather than into the bilge. No leak-prone shaft and stuffing box fittings penetrate the hull. The outboard also offers benefits in boat handling, as demonstrated on the following page.

With all these merits, the outboard does have limitations. In order for the propeller of the short-shafted outboard to stay submerged at all times, the engine can only fit on boats with low transoms—yet a low transom does not always keep out the waves in a following sea. Also, a two-cycle engine burns more fuel for a given horsepower than does a four-cycle. But manufacturers are consistently improving their designs. Most models over 20 horsepower even have provisions for remote controls that allow skippers to control them from a wheel placed forward for greater visibility—a major advantage that was once exclusive to inboards.

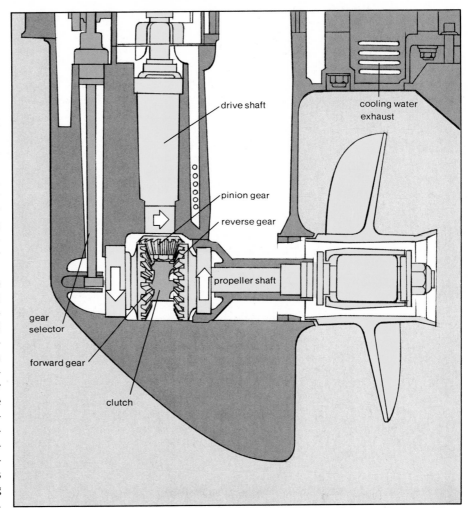

An enlargement of the critical section on an outboard's lower unit shows how the system of three gears can spin the propeller in either forward or reverse. When the engine is running the drive shaft, the pinion gear at its tip and the two connecting bevel gears all turn continually in the direction shown by the arrows. But no power is transmitted to the propeller shaft until the clutch slides to engage one of the bevel gears: the left one is for forward, the right one for reverse.

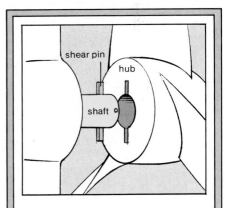

Built to Break

A simple connecting device called a shear (or drive) pin protects the drive train on many outboards. A soft metal rod that locks the propeller hub to the shaft, the pin breaks under the stress of the propeller's striking an underwater object. In large, modern outboards, a slip clutch performs this function.

Pivoting on its mounting bracket, the typical outboard can direct its propeller thrust through an arc of about 70°. Some small outboards can pivot 360°, allowing the boat to go into reverse without changing gears.

The outboard's mounting bracket attaches to the boat's transom by twin C-clamps; between them is a hinge upon which the motor swings, bouncing up over obstructions or tilting up for trailering or beaching.

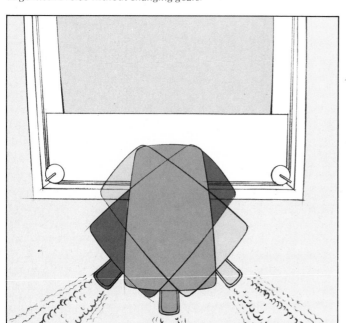

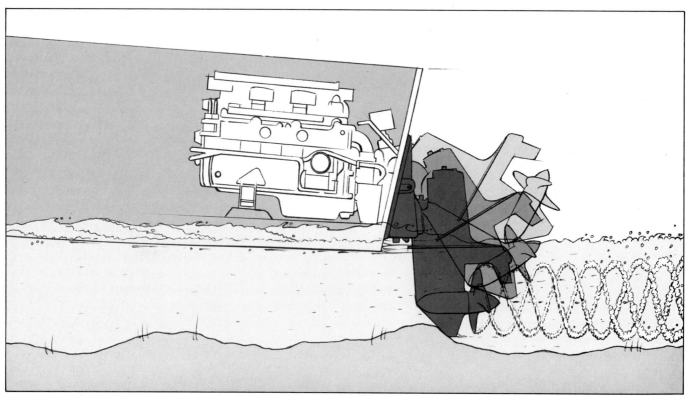

The inboard-outboard (above) delivers the power and efficiency of an inboard, while its outdrive provides an outboard's direct steering thrust and tilts out of the way of obstructions (above). But because its large lower unit stays continually in the water, the I/O is more susceptible to corrosion than an inboard's simple propeller and requires more maintenance than either of its parent designs.

Flexible Power Plants

Although many outboard engines cannot be considered truly portable these days —some 150-horsepower monsters weigh over 250 pounds—they still provide the most versatile and maneuverable power plant a boat can have. They not only propel the boat but also steer it. The simple act of pointing the swivel-mounted engine and its propeller to one side (far left) makes the stern go the other way, and the boat turns quickly in response. With this direct steering thrust, many boats with outboards can turn completely around in their own length.

Another advantage of the outboard is its ability to swing up and out of the water (near left) for beaching, launching, trailering or negotiating shoal waters. Mounted on the transom, the engine is hinged so it can swing back and upward freely. When underway, it is pressed forward into the vertical position by the propeller's thrust. But a shallowing bottom or an underwater obstruction bumps it up and out of danger's way. When the obstacle has been cleared, the outboard settles back into operating position.

Adding to the outboard's versatility is the fact that an owner can fit out his craft with a different power plant simply by unclamping his old motor and installing another. This option can make for trouble, however, if a skipper is tempted to buy more power than his boat can handle; an overpowered boat is a dangerous one. That is why marine engineers have set maximum safe horsepower standards for outboards. Today the Coast Guard requires that all hulls less than 20 feet long carry a plate certifying their rated horsepower capacity. Yet even within these limits the range of outboard power options available to the prospective engine buyer is both wide and flexible, as shown on the chart at right.

Most of the advantages of the outboard motor are shared by an ingenious hybrid, illustrated at left, called the inboard-outboard; it is also known as the I/O or stern drive. The I/O combines the fuel efficiency and power of the four-cycle inboard engine with the maneuverability of an outboard by connecting an inboard engine to an outboard's lower unit through a sizable hole in the transom.

However, the I/Os too have weaknesses, chief among which is the complexity and vulnerability to corrosion of the outdrive unit. Thus it seems unlikely that the stern drive or anything else will soon supplant the ubiquitous outboard as a small-boat owner's best bet for propulsion.

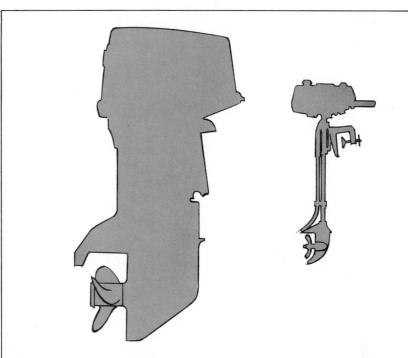

The Right Motor for Your Boat

Outboard motors come in many sizes (above), from pony-power designs that weigh only a few pounds to 150-horsepower brutes that are hardly more portable than some automobile engines. The proper choice of an outboard depends primarily on the size of the boat, its design and the use to which it will be put. Flat-bottomed craft require less power than Deep Vs; water-skiing and offshore fishing demand a high-performance engine, while slow trolling or just poking about in sheltered waters requires no more than a put-put. The chart below indicates horsepower limits for boats of various sizes and hull shapes. Based on industry specifications, the speed and power ranges suggest minimums as well as maximums, since too little power on an outboard hull can hamper its performance.

Type of Boat	Length	Horsepower	Cruising Speed (mph)
Flat-bottomed Utility	9'-12'	4-10	5-15
Flat-bottomed Utility	12'-15'	5-15	5-25
Semi-V Runabout	14'-16'	20-50	20-30
Semi-V Runabout	16'-18'	50-100	25-35
Deep-V Runabout	16'-20'	65-135	25-45
Cathedral Runabout	12'-16'	40-65	20-30
Cathedral Cruiser	16'-20'	65-135	25-40
Semidisplacement Cruiser	18'-24'	85-150	20-40
Houseboat	20'-25'	40-85	10-20
Inflatable Rubber Boat	12'-14'	10-35	15-25
Canoe	15'-17'	1.5-4	3-6
Day Sailer	14'-18'	1.5-5	3-6
Cruising Sailboat	18'-24'	5-20	6-9

5 Once a boatbuilder has designed a hull and the means to drive it, perhaps the toughest challenge to his ingenuity is fitting in everything necessary to keep the crew comfortable and safe. The first builder of record to face this problem was Noah, who had to cram all of the earth's menagerie into an ark of 300 cubits—about 450 feet—in length. Judging from the patriarch's successful stewardship, he must have followed two cardinal rules of naval design: tailor accommodations to a specific task, and make the best use of available space.

No modern pleasure craft, motor or sail, has ever had to undertake the epic task performed by Noah's ark—though in the opulent early days of this cen-

A PLACE FOR EVERYTHING

tury, one owner fitted his steam yacht with an electric horse for an occasional canter at sea. Still, no boat has room enough for everything. Space is particularly tight in today's generally small, compact vessels, and whenever possible each area must do double or triple duty: cabins serve as living rooms by day, dormitories by night and dining rooms at mealtime. Every cranny belowdecks becomes stowage space for passengers' gear or such boat-handling equipment as lines and fenders. One of the beauties of a well-designed boat, in fact, is the skillful marriage of comfort and efficiency that can sometimes be achieved—as in the meticulously appointed mahogany- and teak-trimmed main cabin of the 38-foot yawl *Finisterre (left)*.

In designing the layout of a sail- or powerboat, the seaworthiness of the vessel and the safety of its crew come first. Belowdecks areas, such as the cabin and engine compartment, are equipped with waterproof ventilation devices: hooded or shielded air intakes, leading from deck to compartment, that let air down below and yet keep spray and seawater out. Uncluttered decks, covered with synthetic nonskid surfaces, should be encompassed by life lines. Topside and below, there must be handholds as adjuncts to sea legs in rough going, and corners are rounded to spare bruised hips and dented skulls.

Beyond these precautionary features, a boat's layout will depend on its size, how many people it will carry and what kinds of voyages it is likely to undertake. A deep-water cruising boat, for example, is largely enclosed—containing bunks, a galley for cooking, bathroom facilities (known as the head in proper seaman's usage) and as much storage space as can possibly be sandwiched or shoehorned between, under and behind the boat's basic fixtures. A day sailer or a motor-driven runabout, on the other hand, will be open, with a roomy cockpit and very little else.

Within these extremes lies an extraordinary variety of possibilities for using the boat's interior, and mariners have developed scores of inventive methods for getting the most out of what space is available. The back rests of cabin seats fold up horizontally to become bunks; dinette tabletops lower to bench height, also doing duty as bunks; the top of the icebox serves as the navigator's chart table. A shower may double as a wet locker for the drying of wet suits or foul-weather gear.

Marine designers have also turned their skills to creating special devices that bring a measure of equanimity to housekeeping at sea. For example, to help protect the ship's cook from scalds and burns when the boat heels, stoves can be mounted on gimbals, which are pivoted supports that keep the stove and the pots on it level even in rough conditions.

While such ingenuity helps, the key to efficient use of space in any boat lies in strict application of the principle that all gear, both the boat's and the crew's, be kept where it belongs. An old nautical adage—adapted or perhaps invented independently by a prudent housewife—expresses the principle best: a place for everything, and everything in its place.

Less than 12 feet square, Finisterre's compact main cabin (shown looking aft) includes a table, two bunks, navigation gear, galley and housekeeping equipment for a crew of seven.

Working Space on Deck

Aboard any sailing vessel, large or small, the principal business of a voyage is conducted on deck; thus the topside layout is designed primarily to enable the skipper and crew to sail efficiently and safely.

Headquarters is in the cockpit, sometimes wryly referred to by overworked crewmen as the place where the skipper takes it easy. In fact, even in fairly roomy vessels such as the 32-foot cruising sloop shown here, the cockpit is first of all a working space—and only secondarily is it for relaxing and socializing. Based here, a helmsman—generally the skipper—presides at tiller or wheel, within reading distance of a compass and close to the controls for the auxiliary engine, if there is one. From the cockpit he can make or order all sail adjustments. Winches ease the task of pulling in sails, and the ends of working lines are secured to fastenings called cleats. Cockpit lockers house extra lines, sail bags and other gear.

Forward of the cockpit, deck space is likewise essentially designed for working the boat. The block, or pulley, for the mainsheet—the line that is hauled in or let out to control the mainsail—rides in a track called a traveler. The mast carries winches for raising the sails, which are hauled up with lines called halyards.

The emphasis along the nonskid decks is on safety. The plastic-coated wire life lines are threaded through sturdy metal stanchions designed never to break; under the impact of a 200-pound crewman flung across the deck in heavy seas they may bend, but not fracture. The stainless-steel pulpit on the bow—just above the running lights set on either side of the hull to mark the boat at night for other navigators—will take the same degree of punishment. Grab rails along the cabintop offer extra handholds.

The deck of a sailboat has another vital function: keeping water out of the boat. Scuppers along the toe rail drain away spray and green water. Hatches are battened down firmly underway; cockpit seats have drains to keep water out of the lockers beneath them. The companionway, the access to the space belowdecks, can be a point of peril in heavy weather when a boat might be knocked over on its side. Unless sealed up tight, the boat could swamp. Buttoned up, however, a well-built boat can withstand astonishing punishment. In 1964, in a near hurricane off the South Carolina coast, the yawl *Doubloon* capsized twice in mountainous waves and rolled all the way over both times—but still survived.

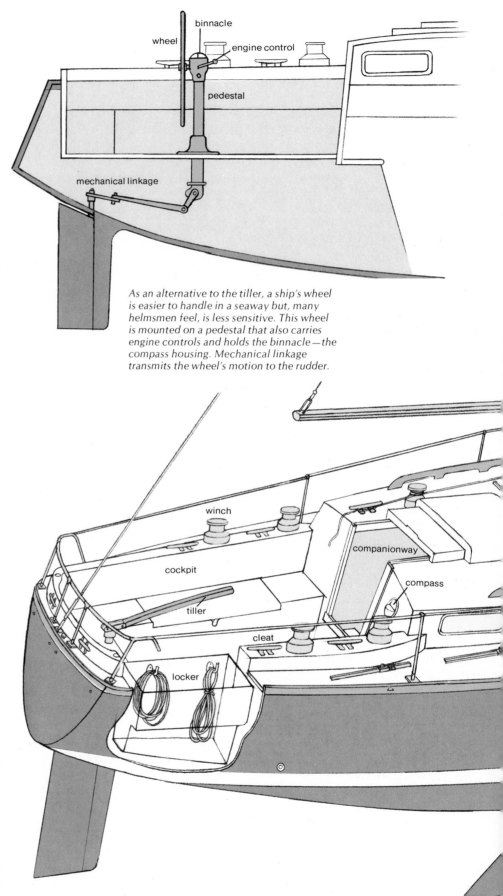

As an alternative to the tiller, a ship's wheel is easier to handle in a seaway but, many helmsmen feel, is less sensitive. This wheel is mounted on a pedestal that also carries engine controls and holds the binnacle—the compass housing. Mechanical linkage transmits the wheel's motion to the rudder.

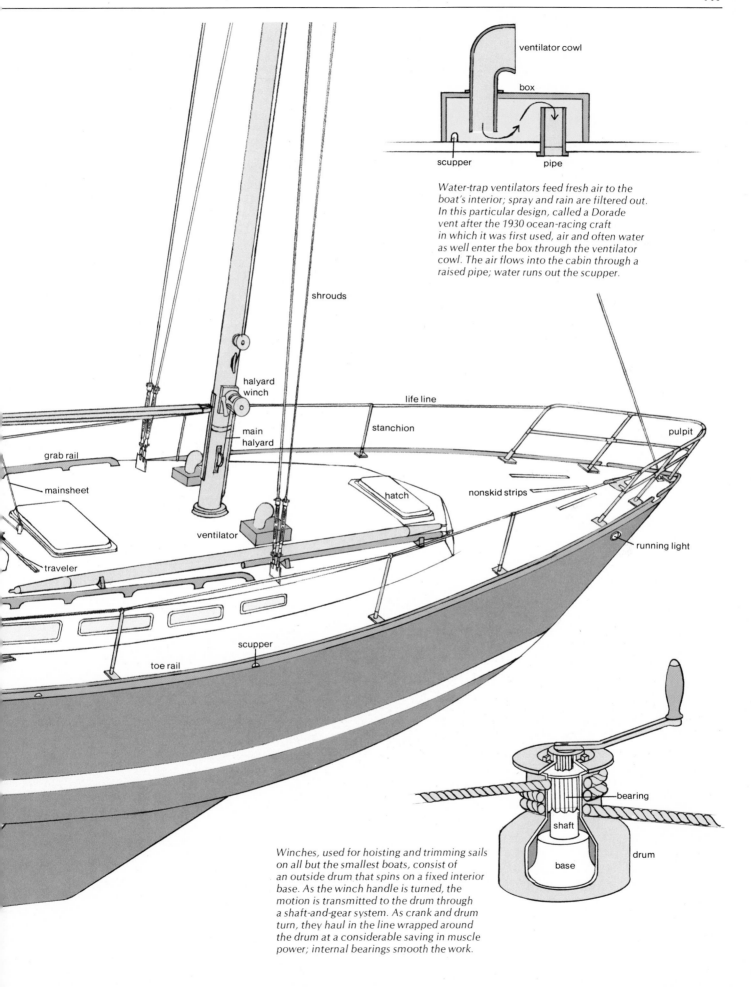

ventilator cowl

box

scupper

pipe

Water-trap ventilators feed fresh air to the boat's interior; spray and rain are filtered out. In this particular design, called a Dorade vent after the 1930 ocean-racing craft in which it was first used, air and often water as well enter the box through the ventilator cowl. The air flows into the cabin through a raised pipe; water runs out the scupper.

shrouds

halyard winch

life line

main halyard

stanchion

pulpit

grab rail

nonskid strips

mainsheet

hatch

traveler

ventilator

running light

scupper

toe rail

bearing

shaft

base

drum

Winches, used for hoisting and trimming sails on all but the smallest boats, consist of an outside drum that spins on a fixed interior base. As the winch handle is turned, the motion is transmitted to the drum through a shaft-and-gear system. As crank and drum turn, they haul in the line wrapped around the drum at a considerable saving in muscle power; internal bearings smooth the work.

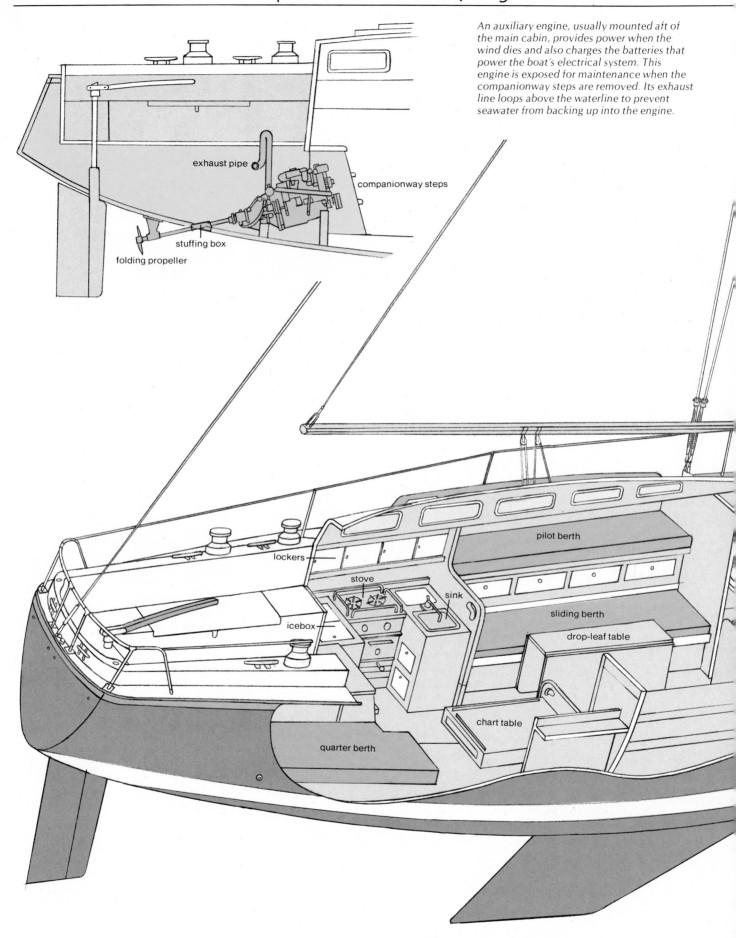

An auxiliary engine, usually mounted aft of the main cabin, provides power when the wind dies and also charges the batteries that power the boat's electrical system. This engine is exposed for maintenance when the companionway steps are removed. Its exhaust line loops above the waterline to prevent seawater from backing up into the engine.

exhaust pipe

companionway steps

stuffing box

folding propeller

lockers

stove

sink

icebox

pilot berth

sliding berth

drop-leaf table

chart table

quarter berth

This galley stove burns alcohol fed to the burners from a tank that is pressurized with air by means of a portable hand pump; a gauge on the tank indicates the pressure level. Gimbals, or pivots, keep the stove level despite the roll of the boat, and a stopcock shuts off the system when not in use.

pressure gauge

detachable pump

flexible hose

stopcock

gimbal

head

berth

hanging locker

handle

rotating valve

mounting pad

hull

All through-hull openings below waterline, such as the head outlet, must be fitted with seacocks as a precaution against leakage. When the handle is parallel with the seacock outlet pipe, as at right, an opening in the cylindrical valve allows water to move through the pipe; setting the handle at right angles to the pipe closes the seacock.

Living Space Below

In 1898 Captain Joshua Slocum anchored in Newport, Rhode Island, to complete an epic 38-month, 46,000-mile, solitary voyage around the world in *Spray*, a sloop only four feet longer than this 32-footer. Slocum's voyage was a classic of spartan seamanship. His chronometer was a one-dollar tin clock and he cooked on a two-burner lamp donated by a Boston lady.

If Slocum were making the same voyage today, his passage would be just as safe and a lot more comfortable in a craft fitted with the modern belowdecks layout shown in this cutaway diagram. This boat crams more accommodations into the main cabin than *Spray* carried from stem to stern. The interior, cozy for four, provides quarters for seven in a pinch. Two single berths in the forward cabin double during the day as storage space for sail bags and life preservers. In the main cabin the two padded fore-and-aft seats can be slid out for spacious nighttime sleeping, while the shelflike pilot berth set back above each seat provides still more bunk room. Tucked in aft on the starboard side is a quarter berth; handy to the chart table, it doubles as the navigator's perch.

In most boats, a degree of privacy can be achieved by closing off the forward cabin—either with a curtain or by swinging open the door to the head. Amenities in the main cabin may include a drop-leaf dining table or one that swings up against a bulkhead to clear the passageway.

Every available space is reserved for lockers to stow food, drink, clothing and other gear. Drawers glide on notched runners to forestall the dumping of their contents during a rough passage. The same messy probability has inspired fiddles—raised edges on tables and countertops.

The placement of the galley—just inside the companionway for easy loading of supplies—is a reflection of the do-it-yourself life style of modern boating. In the days when most yachts carried a paid crew, the galley was just abaft the forward cabin, where the cook slept. Today, when the cook is usually a member of the family, the galley's position puts the stove closer to the boat's center of gravity, minimizing the effects of pitch and roll—and the cook's problems. In this boat, the stove and oven are fueled with alcohol, though some models run on bottled propane gas. Left of the stove stands a compact icebox; larger yachts often carry a refrigerator powered by the craft's electrical system. The sink faucet discharges fresh water pumped from storage tanks under the cabin's sliding berths.

Designed around Power

Blunt and beamy, most powerboats seem roomier than they really are—and this 30-foot cabin cruiser is a case in point. Its compact layout solves the same problems of limited space that confront a sailboat designer: how to fit in all the essentials for efficient seamanship and still leave space for the skipper and crew. Thus the powerboat's superstructure not only must house living quarters but also contain the command post that controls the boat.

Packed into a compartment located beneath the cockpit deck is the heart of the powerboat: the engines. Both heavy and bulky, they must share space with storage batteries and tanks for fuel and water, yet they must also be given enough elbowroom for maintenance and repair. Large deck hatches provide access, and forced-air blowers forestall the breeding of noxious or explosive engine-room gases. As a further safeguard, the law requires that fire extinguishers be installed nearby.

The man at the helm controls the power plant's mechanical muscle. His working space in the vessel illustrated here is on a flying bridge atop the cabin superstructure. That spot is a fair-weather post, protected only by a windscreen; yet the flying bridge offers a singular advantage: 360 degrees of visibility for tight maneuvering at a dock or in crowded sea lanes. Many boats this size also have a second control center that shares houseroom with the living space inside the cabin.

Either post—above- or belowdecks—puts the helmsman within easy reach of throttles, clutches and gauges for controlling and monitoring the vessel's performance. To these basic instruments the captain of a large powerboat may add all kinds of electronic aids—radiotelephone, radar, fathometer, radio direction finder and even electrically operated trim tabs to control the boat's attitude in the water.

Much of this electronic gadgetry runs on its own built-in batteries. Some of it may connect with the ship's electrical system, usually powered by 12-volt batteries charged by the engine. In addition, many boats have a fitting to connect the electrical system to dockside power lines.

Other gear for operating and navigating the vessel is judiciously placed along the decks. A fitting in the foredeck leads to the chain locker, where the anchor line is stowed. Red and green running lights are mounted port and starboard on the rail. A white stern light is affixed to the flagstaff aft, and a rub rail where the topsides meets the deck guards the hull from chafing when the boat is lying at a dock.

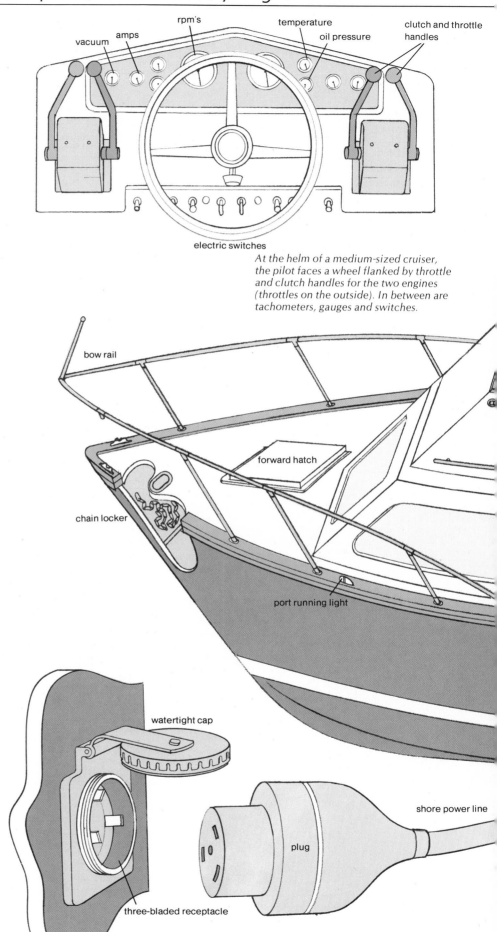

At the helm of a medium-sized cruiser, the pilot faces a wheel flanked by throttle and clutch handles for the two engines (throttles on the outside). In between are tachometers, gauges and switches.

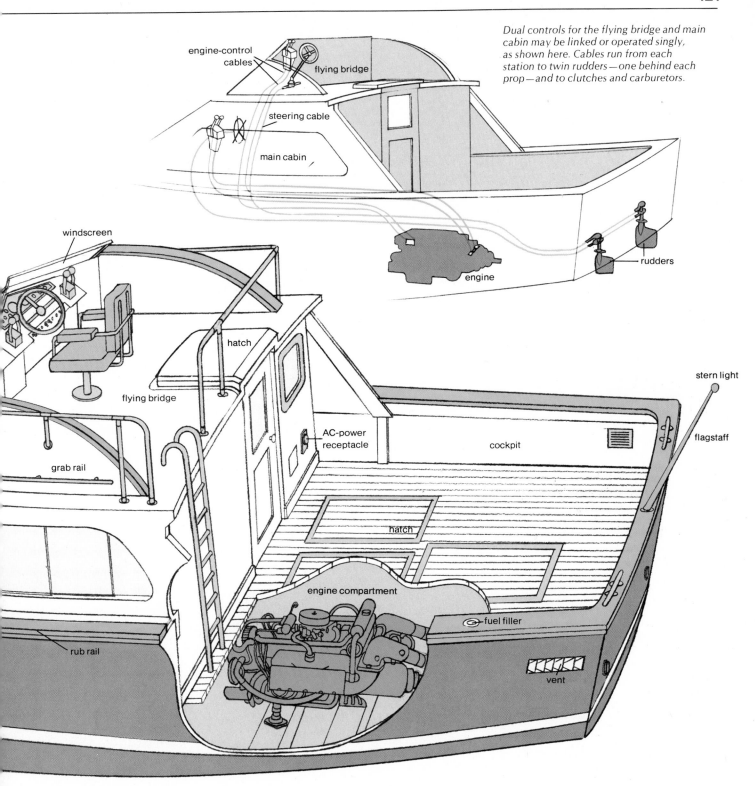

engine-control cables

flying bridge

steering cable

main cabin

Dual controls for the flying bridge and main cabin may be linked or operated singly, as shown here. Cables run from each station to twin rudders—one behind each prop—and to clutches and carburetors.

rudders

engine

windscreen

hatch

flying bridge

stern light

AC-power receptacle

cockpit

flagstaff

grab rail

hatch

rub rail

engine compartment

fuel filler

vent

A plug with a third prong for grounding is the boat's link to dockside power—usually 115 or 125 volts of AC energy. The electricity can be used to run household-type appliances, or it can be channeled through a converter to charge the batteries.

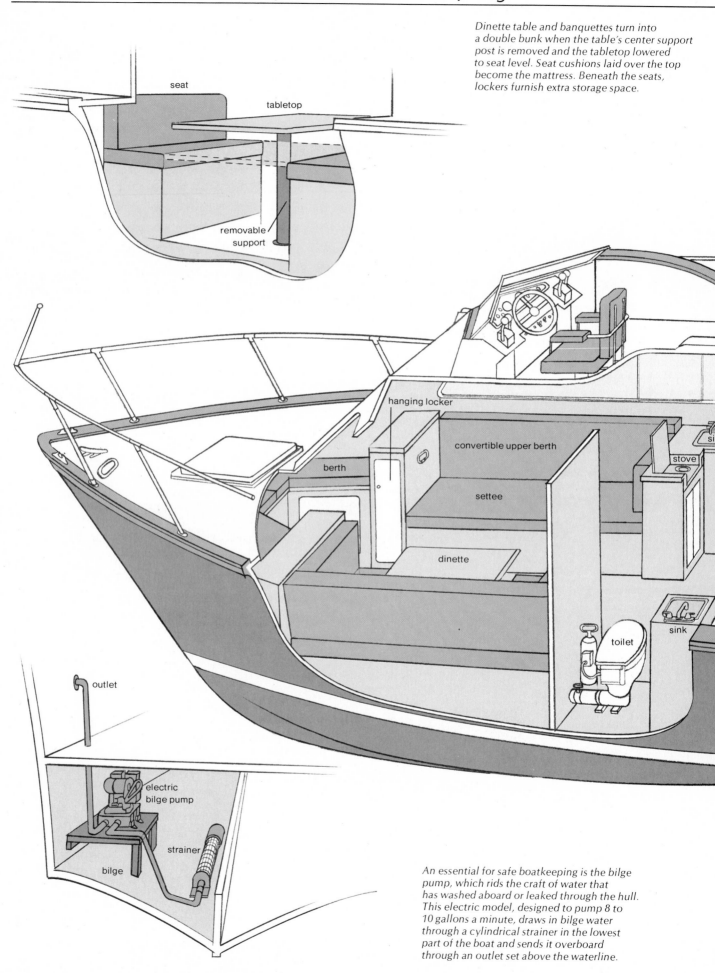

seat

tabletop

removable support

Dinette table and banquettes turn into a double bunk when the table's center support post is removed and the tabletop lowered to seat level. Seat cushions laid over the top become the mattress. Beneath the seats, lockers furnish extra storage space.

hanging locker

berth

convertible upper berth

settee

dinette

sink

stove

sink

toilet

outlet

electric bilge pump

strainer

bilge

An essential for safe boatkeeping is the bilge pump, which rids the craft of water that has washed aboard or leaked through the hull. This electric model, designed to pump 8 to 10 gallons a minute, draws in bilge water through a cylindrical strainer in the lowest part of the boat and sends it overboard through an outlet set above the waterline.

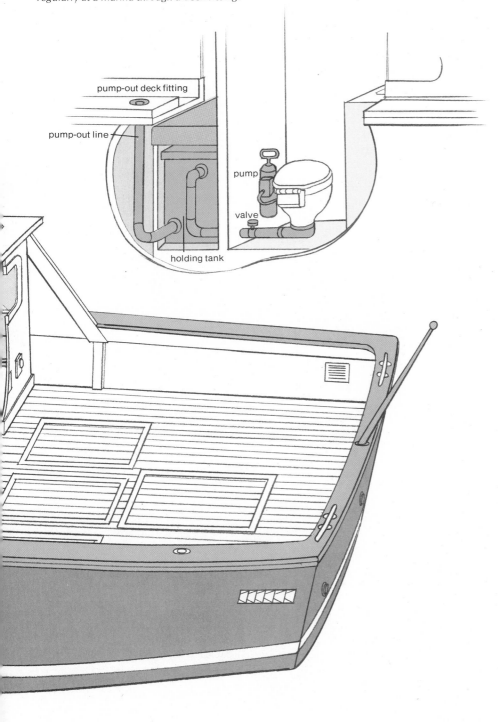

This marine toilet is flushed by a manual pump that takes in seawater, swirls it through the bowl and forces it into a holding tank, which is required by some state laws. Waste collected in the tank is pumped out regularly at a marina through a deck fitting.

pump-out deck fitting

pump-out line

pump

valve

holding tank

Laid Out for Comfort

Shipping out in a modern power cruiser like the 30-footer at left suggests putting to sea in a suburban split-level house—but only barely. To be sure, there is generous sleeping space for six—two in a private stateroom forward and four in the main cabin. The head compartment contains a medicine cabinet, mirror and toilet; the galley has a two-burner electric stove, hot and cold running water and also an electric refrigerator-freezer. The main differences between these water-borne conveniences and their land-bound equivalents are that almost everything is half scale and is packed close together; obviously, some seagoing compromises are necessary to make all these furnishings and appliances fit.

Cabin space becomes a marvel of ingenious compression. The portside dinette unit rearranges into a double bunk. The starboard settee turns into a Pullman-type double-decker when its back swings up to become an upper berth. Stowage space consists of drawers under the seats and berths; port and starboard hanging lockers form the dividers between the forward and main cabins.

For all their close quarters, many powerboats have seagoing amenities that are enhanced by the installation of an auxiliary 115- or 125-volt electrical system, which makes it possible to live the good life aboard with everything from a small refrigerator to air conditioning and TV. The juice may come from an AC generator aboard, or when in port it may be drawn from the dockside power line.

Owners of such electrified craft sometimes carry vacuum cleaners to keep things shipshape. But even without such housekeeping amenities, cleaning chores are minimal thanks to modern furnishing materials—washable laminates, mildew-free vinyl cushion covers and all-weather carpeting. Some manufacturers even lay carpet all the way up the bulkheads to absorb engine noise and vibration.

Beneath all the styling and beautification, however, are some essential boat-keeping fixtures: bilge pumps, seacocks, fire extinguishers and, hidden behind a bulkhead, a holding tank for the toilet. Antipollution regulations in certain areas prohibit dumping household wastes directly overboard; the holding tank, which can be emptied at a marina pump-out facility, helps uphold the rules. Similar arrangements employ a macerater-purifier, which grinds waste into a liquid pulp and treats it with a disinfectant, such as chlorine bleach, to destroy bacteria.

Three Plans for Power

Like many another machine, powerboats need to be especially designed to meet the varying demands put on them. This specialization is graphically apparent in the differing topside layouts of the trio of 18-foot fiberglass models shown here. All three take up an identical amount of space at the dock. But when they cast off they are likely to set out on fundamentally different errands, which give to them their distinctive names: runabout, sport fisherman and overnight cruiser.

The boat at near right, powered by a single outboard, is suitable for water-skiing, sunbathing or speeding around in such sheltered waters as lakes, harbors and bays. The two back-to-back seats can fold flat for sunbathers to stretch out on. Three passengers can occupy the forward bench seats, while half a dozen more—including the helmsman at the wheel on the right—can ride aft. (The traditional location of the steering wheel in powerboats is on the starboard side, where the skipper has a clear view forward and to his right, since the rules of the nautical road require that he yield to another vessel approaching from that direction.)

The twin-engined, center-console outboard at center can be used for sport fishing, offshore scuba diving or as a multipurpose utility boat. Its two engines give extra reliability in case one breaks down in open waters. The midship placement of the skipper's seat, the wheel and the instrument console leaves open passageways on both port and starboard sides for playing a fish. Rod sockets fitted in both gunwales facilitate trolling, and hatches in the raised forward section open to storage compartments and a watertight well for holding fish or bait.

The snugly appointed vessel at far right is a compact overnight cruiser, providing accommodation for two in the forward cuddy cabin, which also encloses storage space and a head. This cruiser carries an inboard-outboard power plant—the engine in the hull powers a geared outdrive mechanism. A windshield and side glass furnish spray protection; some models can also be rigged with convertible tops to ward off sun as well as spray. As a family boat this is among today's most popular configurations.

All three of these boats carry such standard gear as chocks to keep anchor, docking and tow lines from chafing the rail. A combination port-and-starboard running light forward meets federal requirements for motoring at night, as does the stern light mounted on the flagstaff.

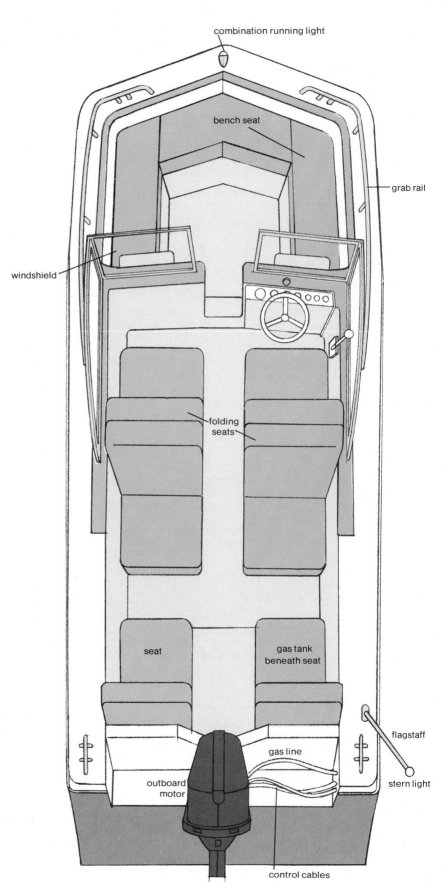

For picnickers and skylarkers, the outboard runabout offers a handy floating playground.

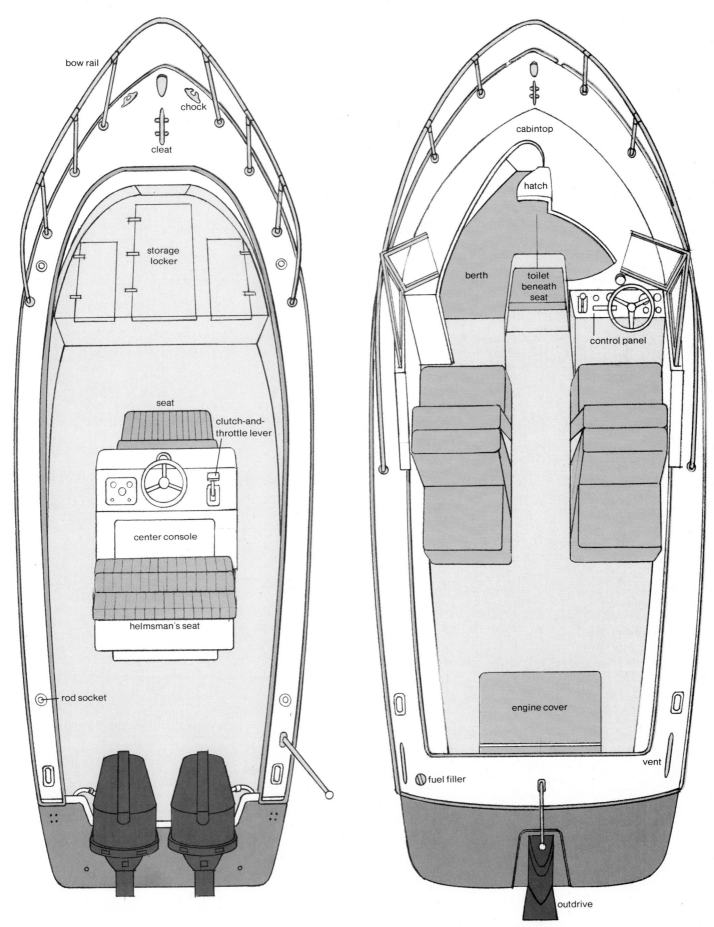

bow rail

chock

cleat

storage
locker

seat

clutch-and-
throttle lever

center console

helmsman's seat

rod socket

cabintop

hatch

berth

toilet
beneath
seat

control panel

engine cover

vent

fuel filler

outdrive

*A deep-water fisherman gets what he needs
here: plenty of power and elbowroom.*

*A mini-cruiser with two bunks forward makes
a cramped but workable overnighter.*

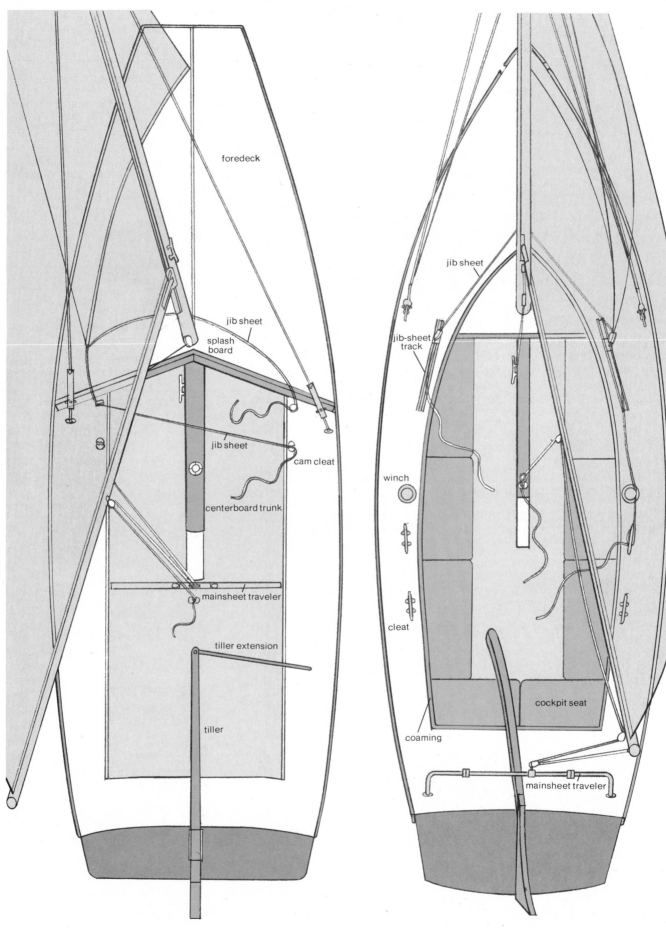

foredeck

jib sheet

splash
board

jib sheet

cam cleat

centerboard trunk

mainsheet traveler

tiller extension

tiller

jib sheet

jib-sheet
track

winch

cleat

cockpit seat

coaming

mainsheet traveler

*This racing craft, demanding spunk and skill,
offers a thrilling ride or a sudden dunking.*

*Ideal for short outings, the roomy day sailer
keeps a small crowd dry and comfortable.*

chock

berth

cabintop

toilet beneath seat

compass

mainsheet

coaming

outboard bracket

Basic cruising comfort, overnight space for two, is squeezed into this mini-yacht.

Three Schemes for Sail

These three sailboats—all 19-footers, all centerboarders, all suited to trailering—are put into the water with significantly different intentions in the minds of their captains and crews. Like the three power-boats on the preceding pages, these craft furnish yet another demonstration that boats are most successful when function dictates configuration.

The square-bowed vessel at far left is a racing sloop, tailored for speed with scant regard for comfort. Its deck hardware is both lightweight and efficient, including quick-release cam cleats for sheets that must be secured or let go in a hurry. The seatless cockpit is only inches deep and except for an abbreviated splash board at its forward end has no water-deflecting coaming—a lack that makes it easy to hike out to windward when the boat heels. (When hiking out, the helmsman controls the tiller with a hinged extension.) A flat bottom enables the boat to get up and plane in even a moderate breeze.

All this ensures a spray-drenched ride, which discourages no skipper attuned to speed and thrills. For here is the sailor's equivalent of a sports car: fast, tender of helm, responsive to the slightest weight shift or wind fluctuation and intolerant of clumsy handling. At any moment the boat may capsize and hurl the crew overboard.

The day sailer at center, deeper hulled and better protected against spray by a coaming around the cockpit, is designed for drier and less rigorous enjoyments. Its capacious cockpit furnishes comfortable bench seats for half a dozen passengers, and space under the foredeck provides ample stowage for spare clothing or foul-weather gear and a dry passage for the pic-nic fixings. Winches help take some effort out of trimming the sails, and convention-al cleats secure the sheets.

The boat at near left is the most com-fortable and utilitarian of the three: a small cruising sailboat, affording week-end sojourns in sheltered coves. Spartan living quarters for two—coupled with re-liability—are its prime virtues. The boat can also carry a light outboard mounted on a bracket astern. The forward cuddy cabin packs in two bunks, a marine toilet and limited cooking facilities. That such basic amenities are enough for dedica-ted cruising enthusiasts was dramatically proven in 1965 by Robert Manry, who sailed his even smaller 13½-foot *Tinker-belle* across the Atlantic alone and later said "... a boat's size has little or no bear-ing on seaworthiness." A bigger craft sim-ply offers more comfort.

Vintage Luxury

Though very few yachts have space to spare, some are big enough to support a degree of luxury, even opulence. A striking example is the 85-foot steel-hulled *Bonanza*, which was built in 1910 and now successfully combines the elegance of an earlier age with the utmost in up-to-date seagoing comfort.

Bonanza has three roomy staterooms and three heads. The original paneled dining saloon has become a lounge, with game tables and television *(below)*. The galley, transplanted from the hold in order to leave space for a laundry, is now amidships; it includes a dining table ample enough to seat the owner, Ted Martin of Bellevue, Washington, his wife and his eight children. A second lounge has a bar, another TV set and a stereo system.

A pair of 150-horsepower diesel engines power *Bonanza*, and a diesel-oil furnace warms her. She even has her own support fleet: two auxiliary craft on board and, in tow, a speedboat for water-skiing.

Elderly but well preserved, Bonanza lies peacefully anchored in a well-sheltered cove during a weekend cruise on Puget Sound.

The forward lounge, located below and just forward of the bridge, retains the mahogany woodwork and the brass clock and lamp fixtures of an earlier era. Here a sturdy captain's table and some smaller ones secured to the deck give the Martin children a quiet spot for refreshments and a game of checkers. Curving under the forward windows is a banquette covered by mildew-proof vinyl upholstery.

Contemporary decorating touches bring a cheerful ambiance to the
aft lounge, Bonanza's main saloon. The stereo system's speakers
hang above the sofa, and a counter at center serves as a bar.
The galley, seen at rear through the door and windows, contains a
propane-gas range with oven, a freezer, a refrigerator that can run on
either gas or electricity, and sufficient dining space for 10.

A guest stateroom below the aft lounge embodies two rare luxuries at sea: roominess and privacy. The living area is amplified by cleverly designed storage space, like built-in bunk drawers with notched runners to keep them closed when the boat rolls.

Younger members of the Martin clan enjoy a snack on Bonanza's afterdeck, or fantail. Fishing poles can be fitted into sockets in the rail for trolling—a favorite Martin sport.

Edwardian elegance enriches the forward cabin, once the dining saloon, which retains the mahogany paneling and cabinetry installed by the builder over 60 years ago. Behind the round captain's table, a sideboard with leaded-glass windows holds books and a TV set.

6 Sooner or later, everyone who enjoys boats wants to stand at his very own helm. If he is a Greek shipping magnate or a Texas oil millionaire, he can satisfy his proprietary itch by ordering up a designed-to-order, hand-assembled floating palace. Less affluent seafarers content themselves with craft already constructed and available through a number of commercial channels. Builders display their products in boatyards and marinas and on the pages of boating publications. Major dealers maintain showrooms where new power cruisers and racing sloops ride resplendent on oceanic expanses of green flooring. The most exciting and varied concentrations of new pleasure

SHOPPING AROUND FOR A BOAT

craft occur at annual boat shows *(pages 148-155)*, where manufacturers and designers proudly launch their latest lines. But for all the lure of the shiny and new, a fledgling purchaser often does better to buy at a used-boat yard.

Not only is a used boat generally cheaper than a new one, but it offers other advantages as well. Joints have worked, seams have closed, engines have been broken in and such new-boat problems as loose fittings and hidden leaks have been discovered and—with luck—corrected. Some boats, like antique cars, even gain value with the years.

With these merits go all the dangers of any secondhand purchase. Simple old age is a problem, but inept usage and careless maintenance by previous skippers is worse. One way to screen out the misfits is to deal through a yacht broker, whose business is to handle vessels in good condition and who knows the fair market price for each model and vintage. The broker can save the boat buyer money by shepherding him through contract legalities and shielding him from sales dodges and hidden charges. The best hedge, however, against buying a secondhand dud is to invest in the expert skill of another maritime professional, the surveyor.

Many used boats, of course, change hands without a surveyor's ministrations; if the buyer knows the boat or its present owner or is enough of an expert himself to do the inspection job, all goes well. Even a knowledgeable buyer, however, takes a considerable risk on his own. Experienced boatmen argue that spending more than a few thousand dollars on a boat without having it surveyed is like acquiring a spouse through the want ads. A corroded shaft that fails at the wrong moment—at sea with a storm brewing—can cost much more than a surveyor's fee, which usually runs about $25 an hour.

In return for his pay, the surveyor warns his client away from an unseaworthy boat disguised under a gleaming coat of paint; he can also spot a poorly kept boat that is still a bargain. He may even veto a perfectly sound vessel if he thinks it is beyond his client's capabilities, which a really expert surveyor takes care to check out along with the boat.

To reach his estimate, the surveyor examines a boat inch by inch, crawling into deck compartments, behind bulkheads, inside bilges and other tight spots—a scrutiny so vigorous that it has led to a boatyard saying: "Never hire a fat surveyor." In the process, he may uncover and diagnose such ills as those pictured on the pages that follow. A good surveyor will also make sure that the buyer knows the true condition of a sailboat's mast, rigging and sails, which may be stored separately and are thus often overlooked. And he will have his client insist on a detailed inventory of what the owner is selling along with the hull: trailer, engine, galley equipment and navigational gear.

In the end, a surveyor can save his client far more than the cost and effort of renovating a broken-down boat. After a group of nuns living near Long Island Sound bought a sailboat for $150, a local surveyor was called to look it over. He told the nuns to burn the boat—and may well have saved their lives.

Sizing up possible purchases, a would-be boatowner listens to marine surveyor John Atkin, who points out the virtues and faults of a secondhand cabin cruiser.

Two serious danger signals appear on the underbody of this 50-year-old sailboat. Rust stains weeping down the keel indicate that the iron keel bolts have deteriorated and need replacing, and the dark discoloration above the keel shows that oil seepage from the engine has decomposed the wood. The shape of the rudder may also indicate trouble: the rounded extension on its upper left-hand edge is an obvious afterthought, suggesting that the boat requires added rudder area because it is hard to steer.

Strips of lead sheathing nailed over this hull planking indicate that the plank ends have come loose and the seams have opened up; such extensive patching is symptomatic of a leaky and generally unsound boat.

Inspecting Wood Hulls

It is an axiom among yachtsmen that a well-made wood boat can last indefinitely, and there are still a few 100-year-old planked hulls afloat to prove it. With hard usage or careless maintenance, however, a wood boat will eventually fall apart. A surveyor's job is to spot the telltale signs of present or future breakdown.

A survey begins with a canny appraisal of the boat's overall shape. Though wood is long lasting partly because of its flexibility under stress, a wood hull can be sprung permanently out of shape if subjected to unnatural strains. For example, the taut shrouds that support a sailboat's mast can eventually lift and permanently deform the boat's midship section, an unhappy phenomenon known as hogging. And powerboats, too, can be misshapen by improper cradling when hauled out. Since such distortions in structure may warp or loosen a vessel's planking, a surveyor next inspects the hull's exterior.

The planking of a sound boat holds its curves and is smoothly joined, and the nails, screws or bolts used to fasten each plank are securely seated. The surveyor can check for loose fastenings by thumping the hull. If a plank gives, vibrates or sounds hollow, or if the caulking that stops up the seams jumps out of place, the fastenings are loose and must be replaced.

An inspection of the seams may also reveal whether a boat leaks. Whenever a boat is kept out of the water for a long time, the wood dries and shrinks, and the seams open. If the openings are narrow and even, they will probably swell shut on relaunching. But if the seams are wide or uneven, the chances of a boat's being watertight are poor. Such flaws can often be corrected by replacing faulty planks or renewing loose fastenings.

But these are stopgaps. If neglect or accident has damaged a boat's interior framing, its problems are more severe—and the vessel may be unsalvageable. The surveyor scrutinizes the timbers, stem and keel for cracks or rot. In a sailboat he examines the ballast keel, looking particularly for signs that the keel bolts are giving way (top left). He taps the bolts inside with a hammer or uses a wrench to back them off slightly; sometimes he finds that the bolts have disintegrated entirely. If a boat in this condition were to encounter rough seas, the keel might drop off and sink—followed by the entire boat.

A surveyor's knife prying into a seam in the hull above the turn of the bilge—where the side of the hull meets the bottom—can wiggle the plank, an indication that it has worked loose. Here the cause is inadequate fastenings—undersized screws used as a shortcut by the boat's original builder. A new owner would have to replace all such screws with longer ones—at prohibitive cost.

At the critical juncture between the hull planking and stem of this heavily used power craft, plank ends show signs of springing loose—signifying probable leaks and serious weakening of the hull's structure.

An isolated patch of dry rot is evidenced (right) by flaking paint and the discoloration of the wood underneath. The cause of the trouble is water that has dripped from a tiny drain hole just above the rotted area.

The punky condition of a powerboat transom (above) signals a severe case of dry rot. The rot developed when water trapped by the chrome-trimmed rub rail—which guards the wood from chafing against the dock— penetrated into the uppermost transom planks; the wood there has become so soft that some of the screws securing the rail and deck fittings are beginning to pull out.

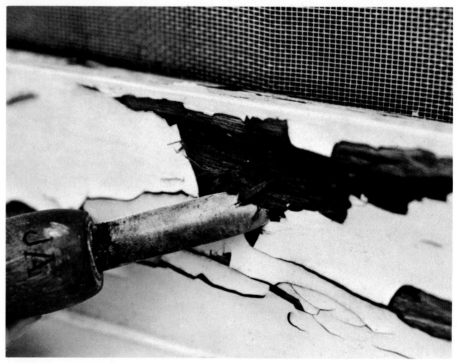

Probing a plank below a screened cabin window, a surveyor's knife reveals how deeply the wood has rotted. The cause is a poorly designed window drainage channel that has let water seep into the wood.

Dry Rot and Wet Glue

"Boats are yare," said Katharine Hepburn to a lubberly companion in *The Philadelphia Story*, "until they develop dry rot." Yare—pronounced yar—means manageable, ready and responsive to the helm. Dry rot means trouble. Paradoxically, dry rot also means moisture.

Wood boats succumb to dry rot as easily as some people catch colds. The condition is an airborne microscopic fungus that attacks moist wood, leaving it in a state of soft, spongy decay. The rot flourishes only where the wood's moisture content reaches at least 20 per cent, and in temperatures of 40° to 100°. It does well in dark and enclosed spaces and finds fresh water more hospitable than salt; in seawater concentrations salt acts to some extent as a preservative. Since the rot needs both moisture and air it will not grow at all if the wood is totally immersed in water; in fact, oldtime fishermen have been known to sink their boats purposely for long periods to kill off the infestation.

Checking for dry rot, a surveyor looks first at areas that tend to trap fresh water: the deck and side planking at the stem and transom, beneath chocks and rails, under drain holes and scuppers.

Inside the hull, the surveyor probes about in any inaccessible, dark area where moist air lingers, such as the ends of beams and frames, along edges of bulkheads, inside lockers, under the ice chest and at the foot of the mast.

If the investigator does not detect dry rot at first sight, he may tap rot-prone areas with a hammer, listening for the spongy sound of decay inside the wood. He can also simply prod—discreetly—with a knife or even a finger, which will sink easily into the rotten wood.

Plywood boats not only are susceptible to dry rot but have a distinct problem of their own: delamination. Plywood consists of thinly sliced sheets of wood glued together under pressure; if the glue used is not waterproof, the layers may simply peel apart, or delaminate, after a boat has been at sea for a while. One way of telling if a hull has been built with top-quality marine-grade plywood—waterproof and knot free—is to look for imperfections in its surface. Inferior material is likely to be patched up with oval wooden inserts, called dutchmen, implanted to replace the surface knots. The surest guarantee, however, is the age of the boat. Any plywood vessel more than 10 years old and still afloat almost certainly is made from the best materials; otherwise it would have long since come unglued.

The drawbacks of inferior plywood are strikingly illustrated on the hull of this boat built of furniture-quality material instead of marine-grade plywood. Three layers of the plywood veneer have peeled off the hull to the left of the keel, leaving only a layer or two between the skipper and the sea.

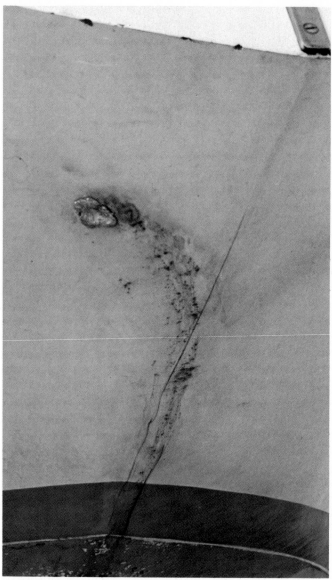

Almost masked by an ugly but harmless stain from the engine exhaust outlet—shown here plugged with metal foil for winter storage—is a crack in the fiberglass hull. The flaw results from the separation of the molded halves of the hull. Running from rudder to transom, the fissure reveals structural damage that may be unsalvageable.

The shape of a fiberglass boat's iron keel mounting is clearly outlined by a pattern of rust—an ominous indication that the mounting has worked loose and is in danger of falling out of the boat. The trouble may have started when the keel hit an underwater rock, levering the mounting—which is not large enough—from its bed inside the hull.

Fiberglass Danger Signs

When fiberglass first appeared as a boat-building material in the late 1940s, it was hailed as a miracle substance that seemed to hold out the promise of total immunity from leaking, cracking, warping or decay. The promise was not fulfilled: fiberglass vessels are subject to all these ills—because of careless maintenance or poor construction. Indeed, so many fiberglass defects result from slipshod manufacture or design that one of the most reliable guarantees of any glass boat is the good reputation of the builder.

Even when new, a fiberglass hull may leak. Water can seep in around fastenings and through-hull fittings. Joints of molded sections may open up, particularly between deck and topsides, cabin and deck, and at the transom. The outer skin, or gel coat, may also contain built-in flaws acquired during the molding process: blisters, bumps, air pockets or sundry other irregularities that weaken the gel coat and sometimes the structure of the hull itself. Even a perfect gel coat, unless periodically waxed or painted, begins to deteriorate after a few years of exposure.

Sometimes fiberglass hulls are simply not made thick enough and are apt to bulge inward under pressure. The surveyor tests for this defect by giving the hull a shove with a knee or an elbow.

One particularly nagging drawback of fiberglass is that it does not hold fastenings with much tenacity, and screws often pull out under stress. Thus the surveyor makes sure that the builder has installed doubling blocks, or wood reinforcements, to securely ground screws or bolts that fasten cleats, rails and other fittings.

A fracture in the fiberglass covering of a cabintop, caused by seagoing stresses, has allowed water to reach wood parts of the structure, which have begun to rot. A leaky cabintop is not unsafe; but this crack is a sign of neglect that may have also affected other crucial areas, such as the hull itself.

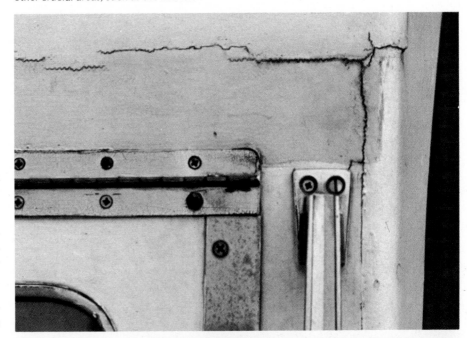

A sprung transom on the outboard above displays a common problem with fiberglass construction: a weak bond between hull and deck molds. An engine too powerful for the boat has caused chafing—which the owner tried to reduce by folding a rubber mat over the transom where the engine mounts.

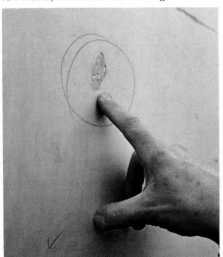

A so-called hard spot—an irregularity in a glass hull's skin—is usually a flaw in manufacture. A few hard spots are not serious; many mean shoddy workmanship.

Despite its shiny topsides and gleaming woodwork this one-year-old homemade ferrocement hull has started to deteriorate, as detailed in the pictures below and at right. The crackling of the paint at the waterline is unsightly, but it is not serious.

A closer look at the hull above reveals hairline stress cracks, a sign the cement has begun to come apart. Such decay could be the result of improper mixing, application or curing of the cement during building.

Below the waterline the ferro-cement hull has a prominent crack—a sign of advanced structural weakening of the cement. Unless both mesh and cement are reconstructed, the boat will be unseaworthy. (Surface mottling is merely flaked antifouling paint.)

Ills of Metal and Cement

Boats built of such seemingly indestructable materials as steel, aluminum and ferro-cement are heir to many of the ills of wood and fiberglass: leaks, loose fittings and structural distortion, for example. They also have a variety of other ailments all their own.

Ferro-cement—an amateur boatbuilder's favorite *(pages 80-81)*—is highly resistant to the ruinous forces of shock, ice, marine life, explosion or fire. But cement boats may contain flaws arising from the combination of rod-and-mesh reinforcement and concrete used in building them. Inadequate metal substructure or poor cement preparation will result in a cracked or crumbling hull like the one at left.

The all-steel sail- and powerboats of today have many of the advantages claimed by ferro-cement craft. Their overwhelming drawback is a seemingly addictive tendency to corrode. One cause is moisture, which encourages rust to form on any unpainted or otherwise unprotected surfaces. When steel starts oxidizing, the best cure is to chip away the corrosion from the blighted area and repaint. Another form of corrosion is galvanic action, an electrochemical phenomenon in which steel reacts with other metals, such as bronze or copper, in the presence of an electrolyte, such as seawater; the reaction causes the steel to be eaten away. Many owners try to eliminate galvanic action by using fittings that will not react with the steel hull. Such precautions help, but they cannot solve the whole problem. Electrical current of any sort will corrode steel: for instance, stray currents from faulty wiring aboard the boat or from improperly grounded dockside power at a marina. So in buying a used boat with a steel hull, it is vital to check how much of the hull is really left. A professional surveyor does this with an electronic device that tests the thickness of the metal plates.

Aluminum boats are lighter than steel ones, strong for their weight and, like all metal vessels, impervious to marine borers and rot—but they, too, can corrode. Paradoxically, one type of aluminum corrosion is not only harmless but actually beneficial; an aluminum surface, when exposed to air and moisture, acquires a thin coat of aluminum oxide that protects the metal from the kind of chronic blight that eats away steel. But even aluminum will corrode if coupled with the wrong metals; and flaws in the metal itself may cause pockmarks like those mottling the area near the propeller of the aluminum hull on the opposite page.

A jagged hole near the keel shows where the steel hull of a $50,000 cutter has rusted all the way through. The aperture had been hidden under a layer of marine plaster, applied years earlier to improve the underwater lines of the vessel's stern. During a routine insurance appraisal, a surveyor found evidence of rust near the rudderpost, gave the area a tap with his hammer and broke clean through: only the plaster surfacing had kept the boat afloat. The hole can be fixed—at great cost—by removing the rusted area and welding in new steel.

Two common forms of corrosion have attacked the surface of this aluminum hull. Neither is as destructive as the rust that gnaws at steel, and one is actually beneficial: an overall dulling of the finish, typical of the aluminum oxidation that protects the metal from further attack. The other type is a pitting of the metal around the propeller, possibly caused by impurities in the alloy. Here the pitting is not particularly alarming, confined as it is to an area that does not carry much stress. But extensive pitting all along the hull would mean costly trouble.

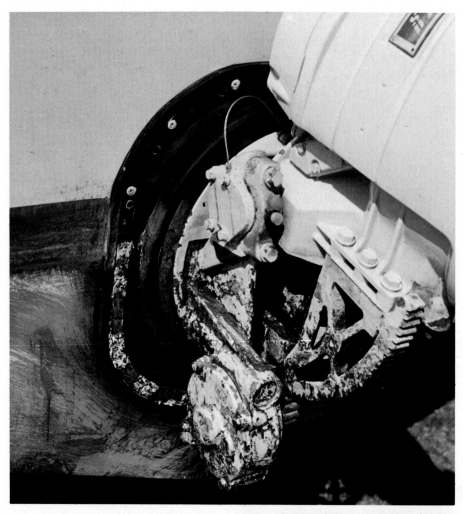

Patches of decay mar the most vulnerable part of an inboard-outboard engine installation: the flexible rubber collar, or boot, surrounding the drive mechanism where it penetrates the hull. The boot, which ensures a watertight fitting, hardens and cracks from exposure to sun and salt water and needs periodic replacement; normal life span is about two years. The engine itself is sound, but the paint scaling off the tilt-up mechanism should be stripped and renewed.

Rust has seized up a small gear in the tilt-up system of an inboard-outboard engine like the one shown at the top of the page. The gear has corroded because it is made of a metal different from—and thus galvanically at odds with—the larger gear. The small gear needs changing—an easy procedure but one that will have to be repeated unless the new gear is made of a metal different from the original.

Other Trouble Spots

If an automobile's engine were banged around and drenched with salt spray like a standard outboard motor, auto repair shops would be more crowded than the highways. On any mechanical equipment aboard a boat, parts rust from water and moist air or corrode when galvanically incompatible metals are fitted together. Propellers erode and snag on the buoy lines of lobster pots, engine outdrive units break down and through-hull connections deteriorate—common defects that are highlighted on these pages.

It is no wonder, then, that marine engines have a limited life span—about 10 years for a gasoline engine, nearly twice as long for a diesel. A survey of any secondhand engine begins by comparing its intended working life with its chronological age. In addition, the surveyor glances at a gauge, usually near the tachometer, that tells him how many hours the engine has been used. A running time of 500 hours is the normal limit before most high-speed power plants must be sent to the shop for a complete overhaul.

In a powerboat or an auxiliary sailboat, the general conditions inside the engine compartment often reflect the health of the engine itself. If the engine housing is clean, the bilges dry, the hose connections secure and rust free, the beds and mounts solid, chances are that the engine itself has also had fastidious upkeep. By the same token, oil in the bilges, sea strainers that are clogged or exhaust lines that leak are signs that the power plant may be in a similarly dilapidated state.

When a boat is out of the water the surveyor examines the propeller to check its external condition, looking for corrosion, bent blades and just plain wear *(right)*. Also, by rotating the propeller manually, he can discover if the shaft has too much play, whether it has seized up or has been damaged and is out of alignment.

Problems of the steering machinery—rusty cables *(far right)*, broken or missing rudder fastenings, a bent or stiff rudderstock—are all easily diagnosed by inspection and are usually fixable. The stuffing boxes, one each where the rudder and the propeller shafts pass through the hull, should be examined to see that they are full of oiled material, called packing, that is resilient and fresh.

Sailboat auxiliary engines should get the same thoroughgoing check-out, especially those parts hidden in enclosed spaces, like the exhaust line that is shown on page 144 as part of an added gallery of areas to be examined with an eagle eye.

Hard use has worn out the complex support mechanism of a stern-drive assembly—two hinged rings that let the outboard unit swivel up and down and from side to side. The inner ring, cracked at its pin, could fall off, taking the outboard unit with it. The whole mechanism must come off so the broken ring can be replaced.

No longer sound, a steering cable—part of the mechanism that allows an outboard engine to be operated from a cockpit wheel—has lost much of its protective covering. The sheave, or pulley, over which the cable runs also needs renewing: it has begun to rust and might bind up or simply break.

This bronze propeller has been severely worn by erosion from sand particles suspended in seawater and by corrosion resulting from a galvanic reaction with the iron strut that holds the prop in place. Other ailments that plague propellers include bent blades and bent or misaligned shafts.

Hidden danger spots to be scrutinized in any boat are the hard-to-reach places where hoses, pipes and cables lead along the hull's interior. In the picture above, the black exhaust hose of a sailboat's auxiliary engine, en route to its through-hull outlet, drips exhaust residue at the point where it passes through a plywood bulkhead in the lazarette, a stowage compartment in the stern. Chafing against the plywood has ruptured the hose. The total damage is revealed by a look at the other side of the bulkhead (above, right), located just below the helmsman's seat, where the plywood has begun to rot.

The patina covering these bronze halyard winches indicates disuse but should not alarm the boat buyer: this natural protective coating is a characteristic of high-quality metal. Before the winches are used, however, their moving parts should be overhauled.

A loose screw in the base of this life-line stanchion calls for a minor but vital repair. The screws should be replaced by longer ones or, better yet, by bolts run through a wood block under the deck; in rough weather a firm stanchion could save a crewman's life.

Damage to a mast usually means a new one must be bought—at major expense. This aluminum spar from a 26-foot boat was bent at the spreaders in a collision: its unrigged replacement cost about $300. To rig and step the new mast will add still another $400.

An improperly glued plastic deck covering, applied to protect the wooden deck planking, has let moisture seep through and rot the wood underneath. Such plastic coatings have become a common way to spruce up old wood boats, and a buyer should make sure they do not mask serious defects.

A Surveyor's Check List

A professional surveyor follows a step-by-step procedure that begins with an assessment of the hull's seaworthiness. He looks for structural distortion and tests the soundness of wood planks, metal plates or fiberglass laminate. Next he goes below to inspect interior framework and fastenings. He examines mechanical and electrical gear, plumbing, and, finally, rigging and sails. The check list presented here, based on this professional approach, will help an amateur boatman make his own evaluation of a new or used craft, with a more discerning eye.

HULL: EXTERIOR	
Structural Condition	From a distance, scan the hull's overall profile for signs of distortion, sagging or hogging—noticeable most clearly at the sheer line, the turn of the bilges and, on a sailboat, amidships where the shrouds are secured. Then explore the hull's surface for the kinds of flaws that sometimes indicate weakened structure: sprung planks on a wood boat, ridges or hollows in fiberglass. On steel or aluminum boats, check for large dents—or superficial plaster patches covering such damage.
Wood Boats: Planking, Fastenings and Seams	Look for corroded or missing fastenings by checking the planking; loose or uneven planks suggest faulty fastenings. So, too, does flaking paint, loose caulking or popped bungs (wood plugs that cover countersunk fastenings). Pay particular attention to stress points, such as the stem, keel, bilges and stern. Next, carefully examine the planks themselves for splits and dry rot; look for wide, uneven seams, indicating that the planks have shrunk and will not swell up uniformly to make the hull tight when the boat is launched. Note excessive patching or repairs, suggesting a leaky or severely damaged hull.
Fiberglass Boats	Examine the gel coat for chafe, blisters and voids. Look for cracks and fractures in the laminate, particularly at the stem, keel, the turn of the bilge, and for separation at the transom of outboard motorboats. Press against the hull; if it buckles, the fiberglass laminate is too thin.
Metal and Cement Boats	Check the plates of a metal hull for dents, abrasions and corrosion, particularly where the paint has chipped; inspect the seams and welds to make sure they are tight. On a ferro-cement hull look for cracks that indicate the mortar was not properly mixed or cured during construction. Note streaks of rust, suggesting deterioration of the internal metal framework.
Keel or Centerboard	Inspect lead ballast on the keel for weak fastenings and damage due to stress or grounding. These defects are revealed by looseness where the keel joins the ballast on wood boats, by cracks or separation on fiberglass or ferro-cement boats and by bending or distortion on metal ones. Rust stains suggest keel bolts may be rusting away. On centerboarders check both the board and the centerboard trunk for chafe and rot. Inside the boat check both the centerboard's pivot pin and pennant, and look for signs of leaking at the foot of the trunk.
Through-Hull Fittings	Examine all through-hull fittings—water inlets and outlets, propeller and rudder shafts—for damage, wear or corrosion. Rotate prop and move rudder to check the alignment of their shafts and the condition of their bearings.
TOPSIDES AND DECK	
Wood	Inspect topsides and deck for damaged or loose planks. Look for dry rot, particularly at places where moisture can collect: around deck fittings and hatches, at the juncture between cabin trunk and deck, along rails and coamings and at the stem and the transom. When decks are plywood, check also for signs of buckling or delamination.
Fiberglass, Metal and Cement	On fiberglass boats look for separation of major joints, such as where the deck meets the hull and the cabin trunk meets the deck. Note any cracks or crazing—indicating stress—around joints or fittings. When fiberglass surfacing has been laid over wood decks, watch for shrinkage, separation or disintegration of fiberglass decking material, which leads to rotting of the wood beneath. On steel and aluminum boats, look for rust and corrosion around deck fittings; check topsides and decks of ferro-cement boats for cracks.
Deck Hardware and Safety Equipment	Make sure chocks, cleats and winches are firmly secured; test winches to see if they turn easily and smoothly. Check for dried-out sealant around bolts or screws; dry, shrunken sealing compound permits leaks. Examine the anchor and chain or rope for damage, corrosion and wear. Inspect safety gear—toe and hand rails, stanchions and life lines—for placement, strength and fastenings; also check life lines for fray or looseness.

HULL: INTERIOR

Structural Members	In a wood hull check frames and other structural supports for fractures, splits and rot. Look for cracks in fiberglass and ferro-cement hulls and for corrosion in metal ones. Note those areas subject to vibration or impact: along the keel, the turn of the bilges, the engine bed, the stem, counter and transom.
Interior Fastenings	Check wood hulls for loose, missing or corroded fastenings, especially at sharp turns where the hull is subject to structural stress. Observe keel bolts for rust. Check fiberglass bonding where bulkheads and other stiffeners join the hull. Examine metal plating for corrosion, particularly at through-hull fittings.
Overhead Seams and Sealants	To make sure overhead seams are watertight, soak the deck and cabin housing with water; loose planking, deteriorated sealant or worn-out decking material will let moisture seep into the cabin. Examine leak-prone areas like hatches, ventilators, deck attachments and mast openings. (Leaks in a boat's bottom are harder to detect when the boat is hauled, but show up clearly when the vessel is launched.)
Ventilation	Confirm that there are enough ventilators and air ducts to allow a free flow of air below decks, particularly in enclosed areas like the forepeak, lockers and head, and between interior paneling and the hull.

MECHANICAL AND ELECTRICAL SYSTEMS

Steering and Controls	Make sure the bridge and cockpit controls are conveniently located and provide good visibility. Inspect steering cables and rods, couplings, gears, wheel or tiller, and rudderstock—the shaft that connects the rudder to the steering gear—for wear, looseness or metal fatigue. In the steering cable look for kinks or fraying; make sure any sheaves, or pulleys, are solidly attached to the hull.
Engine	Note the engine's age and the running time (recorded on the engine-hour indicator) and estimate the interval since its last overhaul. Inspect major visible components—such as the propeller shaft and coupling—for wear and corrosion. Inspect the coolant system, including pump intakes and sea strainers. Make sure exhaust pipes and flexible hoses do not chafe or leak and are insulated where necessary. Examine the engine mounts for wear and misalignment. Find out where the fuel tank's vent is located. Check installation of safety equipment—flame arrester, fire extinguisher, gas detector and blower for venting fumes.
Electrical System	Inspect all wiring, terminals and clamps for fraying, loose connections and corrosion. Ensure that the battery is securely mounted in a ventilated and covered battery box. Make sure that all electrical gear is well grounded, that ground plates are securely attached and that the running lights work and are not corroded.
Plumbing, Head and Galley	Be certain that all pipes and hoses are tightly connected, free of leaks and large enough for the water or waste flowing through them. Test seacocks to ensure that they are not corroded shut and that they are accessible and do not leak. Test the working condition of head, galley and bilge pumps. Water and fuel tanks must be securely fastened and free of leaks or corrosion. Inspect the stove's fuel line, and make sure the fuel supply is ventilated. Look for rot near the icebox drain.

SPARS, RIGGING AND SAILS

Spars	Examine wood masts for distortion, rot and chafe—especially at the heel of the mast and around mast fittings. Check aluminum spars for corrosion, distortion or damage. Look for signs of wear on blocks, sheaves and winches.
Rigging	Inspect all wire stays and shrouds for wear or corrosion, especially at the ends where they attach to fittings, such as shackles and turnbuckles; check the fittings themselves for wear, corrosion or fractures. Examine halyards and sheets for frayed areas. Check deck fittings to see that fairleads, cleats and winches are correctly positioned and securely fastened.
Sails	Find out the quantity, make, year and fabric of sails. Inspect fabric for stretch, chafe and mildew, and look for frayed stitching.

A SHOWCASE FOR NEW BOATS

For those whose yen to buy a boat can be satisfied only with a new model, the boat show is like a candy store to a hungry child. In its glossiest big-city form the boat show is a marine catalogue that offers vessels ranging from sailing prams to 60-foot gold-platers and accessories from saltwater soap to turbo-charged engines.

But the boat-show pageant travels far beyond the big cities. It sets up in towns, villages, even shopping centers all across a boat-happy nation. The show's carnival appeal is apparently limitless; new ones blossom annually, attracting new thousands, some looking for their dream boat, some simply gaping.

The show has a long history: the first large-scale pleasure-boat exhibition was held in New York City in 1905 to demonstrate that craft powered by internal-combustion engines would stay afloat. The event drew 26,000 skeptics to the shores of an artificial lagoon in Madison Square Garden and made believers of enough of them to establish the boat show as a permanent midwinter affair.

Like the powerboat it introduced, the show's appearance has changed through the years: the most recent innovations are specialized shows for power and sail, a trend toward outdoor, in-the-water displays and an extended season that runs nearly year round. But the show's basic function has remained the same—to stimulate consumer interest in the products of the marine industry.

Indeed, the exhibition furnishes a valuable service to consumers. But there are practical limits to a show's value as a marketplace. Though offering a splendid opportunity to compare costs and features of competitive boats and hardware, most shows provide no means by which to test performance. Accordingly, the show is usually a better place to browse than to buy, a place where the search for a new boat is better begun than ended.

Showgoers inspect a 33-foot cabin cruiser placed in a commanding position at the National Boat Show in New York City's Coliseum. Surrounding the cruiser is the shiny array of brand-new speedboats, fishermen, sailboats and dinghies that make this event, an annual fixture for seven decades, one of the season's most popular shows.

Displayed to emphasize their versatility, the boats in this fleet of six runabouts and one small cruiser at the Los Angeles boat show vary only slightly in size, yet each tempts the buyer with a different combination of features. Spanning a cost range of about $5,000, this collection offers a choice of several hull designs, outboard or stern-drive power, and half a dozen seating and decor arrangements.

A squadron of cruiser bows breasts a sea of carpet at the New York
Coliseum. The line-up is still another example of the tantalizing
choices that confront the prospective buyer at a show. Though the
boats all have similar fiberglass hulls, each one is a different length,
from 24 to 38 feet, and each has a different layout—and price.

Like a carnival midway, these Los Angeles boat-show booths entice
visitors with provocative displays, including a gaudy exhibit
of life preservers (center, right), a seductive line-up of marine toilets
(center), intriguing stern propulsion packages (center, left)
and a tempting collection of electronic equipment (foreground).

Closing the Deal

Standing on a powerboat's lofty flying bridge, well above the boat-show bustle and confusion in New York's Coliseum, a shopper and a salesman discuss the fine points of the luxury-equipped cruiser.

Although many boats are sold at boat shows, the sales are usually to skippers who go to such exhibitions with their minds made up. The majority of prospective owners prudently do not sign any sales contracts at the show, but sift the mass of impressions gained there and then carry the search further to dealers' showrooms at local marinas and boatyards before making a final choice.

Once the shopper has narrowed the field to the boat that is right for him—and for his pocketbook—he is still only halfway to his goal. Between the showroom and that first satisfying spin with the family on the water lies a thicket of negotiations. Before taking delivery of the boat and writing out his check, the purchaser should make sure that he will get an in-the-water trial of the new boat. He should also come to a firm understanding with his dealer that the total cost includes all the equipment and accessories needed: every manufacturer has a different idea of what constitutes necessary equipment, and the buyer must be sure that items like sails, lights and bunk cushions will be aboard when the boat arrives.

Delivery arrangements and fees must be established ahead of time. If the freight charges seem high, they should be carefully checked with both factory and carrier. Delivery charges sometimes include the price of a shipping cradle—which a purchaser may end up having to buy regardless of whether or not he needs to keep the cradle for storing the boat.

The extent of the dealer's commissioning service—his contribution to getting the boat ready for the water—and the fee for that service should also be determined ahead of time. Depending on the boat and dealer, commissioning can add several hundred dollars to the cost of an offshore cruiser, or at the other extreme it may be a courtesy included in the purchase price of a utility outboard boat.

Finally, on delivery day the new owner should not accept the vessel until he has inspected it carefully himself—and this includes the agreed-upon test run. Fittings and joints should be evaluated, appliances and instrumentation tested. The hull should be examined for flaws in materials and finish—particularly minor items like paint, varnish and gel coat; since these details are seldom covered by a warranty, this is the last chance to get them fixed for nothing. Indeed, as the chart at right makes clear, the costs of owning a boat are high enough without having to pay for someone else's errors.

Boat-Show Strategy

Most boat-show visitors end up with sore feet and an armload of brochures. While the aching feet may be inevitable, a little strategy can help you get something more than brochures for your pains.

Go on weekdays during work hours to beat the crowd; on weekends, morning is best. Wear comfortable shoes—no high heels.

See every exhibit that interests you; if one is crowded at the first look around, come back. If an appointment is required, make one.

Take notes as well as brochures. Don't be intimidated by salesmen; they are there to inform you. Have you asked about the warranty, the location of dealerships and service, delivery charges?

Evaluate quality of installations and assembly. Boats at the show should reflect the factory's best effort. If you find a lemon here, there is no reason to expect to find peaches in the rest of the line.

Be careful of deals on floor-display boats. Is the craft considered new or used? Who pays to move the boat off the showroom floor? Can you cancel the deal if the craft fails a water trial?

The Continuing Cost of Ownership

Anyone who plans to buy a boat should carefully consider the fact that the purchase price is only the tip of a financial iceberg, as any veteran boatowner who has kept track of his expenses can testify. Some of the costs are unavoidable, some depend on the owner's susceptibility to glittering nonessentials, but rule of thumb suggests that the annual cost of operating and maintaining a boat will be at least 10 per cent of its original price and could range as high as 30 per cent. Within that spread, there are many variables in the cost of ownership: the size and type of the boat; where it is used; and how and by whom. As for where the money goes, the chart below breaks down the bad news into seven categories.

Mooring, Dockage and Storage	The yearly tab for keeping a boat in or near the water at a marina or club during the season, and in dry storage during the winter, can average 5 per cent or more of the vessel's original retail price. Typical fees for slip space range from two to five dollars per foot per month, with the lowest rates usually found at public facilities; indoor dry storage averages around $10 per foot for a season, though outdoor dry storage generally costs 20 per cent to 40 per cent less. Hauling, launching and winterizing may be separate costs. Keeping a boat on a trailer and towing it home after each use will eliminate most of these expenses —though the trailer and towing gear require a sizable initial investment.
Supplementary Equipment	Some new boats come better equipped than others. Gear that should be aboard, but may have to be bought separately, includes life jackets, fire extinguishers, anchor, dock lines, fenders, foul-weather clothing, spare engine parts, and, for small boats, a paddle or an oar. Cost of special gear for racing, water sports and navigation can amount to half again the boat's price.
Maintenance and Repair	Expenses in this category can easily amount to 5 per cent of the boat's original price each year. Typical services and fees: engine checkup ($25 and up); stepping a mast ($25 and up); cleaning of hull (about $1.25 per foot); painting of hull ($1.25 per foot a coat plus materials). Beyond the cost of replacement parts, skilled labor for repairs in many yards starts at $15 per hour.
Insurance	As a rule, the annual cost of comprehensive small-boat insurance ranges between 1.5 to 5 per cent of the purchase price. Small-boat liability coverage is often provided by existing homeowner insurance policies, which may reduce costs in this area. Some boat policies offer discounts for such factors as safety equipment, courses taken by the owner in boat handling, diesel instead of gasoline fuel. Buying insurance for large yachts is more complex: each policy is custom-built and rates can vary widely.
Registration Fees and Taxes	All powerboats must be registered with either state or federal agencies, but the fees seldom run more than $15 for craft under 40 feet; bigger boats mean higher fees. In states that impose personal-property tax assessments on boats, the yearly cost may be substantial.
Operating Expenses	Wind is cheap, so this expense category applies mainly to powerboatmen, for whom fuel economy is the major consideration. Costs vary according to size, design, engine type, speed, weather and skipper: an outboard-powered runabout might consume four to seven gallons of fuel per hour, while a 36-foot twin-screw cruiser might average 15 gallons.
Contingencies	Every season, a fraternity of chagrined boatmen curse the submerged log that mangled a propeller, weep salt tears over a bent aluminum mast or have to hire a diver to retrieve an outboard engine. Such contingencies are almost unavoidable, and they inevitably cost as much in cash as in frustration.

7 Every year, as more and more Americans take to the water, the ways and means for keeping a boat have also proliferated—of necessity. Not so long ago a boatowner could simply set a mooring in the water at a convenient and protected spot. Otherwise he tied up at the town dock. Or he could join a yacht club where—in return for his yearly dues—he got a clubhouse, regattas and a social life along with launch service to his permanent mooring.

But the growth of recreational boating has been so explosive that the berthing space available in the past no longer suffices. Shorelines are becoming overcrowded. Only the man with shore-front property can hope to moor his

WHERE TO BERTH A BOAT

boat at the end of his lawn—and even then he may have to obtain permission from local authorities. Town docks are full, and thriving yacht clubs have had to limit memberships. This shortage of boatkeeping facilities, long a problem on the West Coast, where there are few natural harbors, now afflicts the eastern seaboard and inland lakes. To ease the crowding, a number of boatkeeping arrangements have developed.

The most widespread approach is to remove the boat from the water entirely. The family craft can be kept right at home, just like the family car, because the modern boat trailer *(overleaf)* provides both berth and wheels to haul the boat to water. Though boat trailers are not new—one designed in the 1860s was basically an ox-drawn cart—they were not mass-produced until the 1930s. Today, there are more than three million. Their prevalence has inspired a new design concept, the so-called trailer-sailer equipped with fold-down mast, removable rudder and retractable keel *(page 50)*. Increasing use of trailers has also inspired some state legislatures to pass regulations for highway trailering; local requirements can be checked by calling the state police or highway department.

Another change that the trailer has brought to boating is a new kind of yacht club, democratic and free wheeling: the communally owned boat club *(pages 160-161)*. These groups provide the means for getting a boat into the water as quickly as possible and usually little else. Some have their own launching ramps and clubhouses; others maintain no permanent waterfront facilities at all. Typical of this new breed of boating club, the Clear Lake Sailing Club of Houston, Texas, runs weekly races with no equipment but a homemade pier for rigging the sailboats, a plywood committee boat, a horn and a set of flags. Annual dues are $10 per family.

Such organizations are enormously popular. In 1961 the central states of Kansas, Arkansas, Oklahoma and Missouri could muster a grand total of six boat clubs; 13 years later, well over 1,000 boats sailed out of 22 clubs based on the lakes of the area.

Matching the growth of the private boat club has been the rise of the marina, the public boat basin that is in effect a modernized version of the old town dock. The marina rents its slips by the day, week or season—indeed, in many marinas, such as Manhattan's 79th Street Boat Basin on the Hudson River, tenants live on their boats permanently. Marinas generally charge by the length of the boat. The cost is quite high, but the facilities usually include such useful services as pump-out stations for the boat's holding tanks, gas pumps and showers. Probably the world's most spectacular example of this genre is the Marina del Rey in California's Santa Monica Bay *(pages 164-167)*, whose 5,800 berths make it the size of a small town—which indeed it is, for its boating tenants may also avail themselves of such amenities as shops, tennis courts, swimming pools, parking garages and both permanent and transient onshore living quarters.

A lone boat moored on a quiet lake sums up many a boatowner's dream of boatkeeping; but today's sailor is more likely to keep his craft on a trailer at home or tied up in a marina.

Boats on Wheels

A 15-foot planing speedboat rests on a trailer in its owner's backyard. Mounted on the trailer tongue, a winch for launching and hauling out sports a bright red housing. Keeping a boat in storage on a trailer simplifies maintenance: algae and barnacles do not accumulate on the hull, and moisture is less likely to corrode mechanical parts.

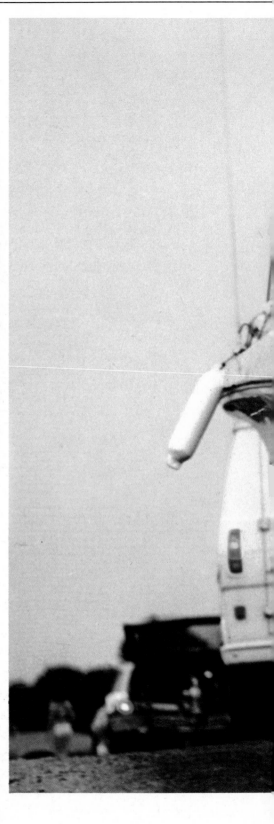

At a seaside launching ramp, a small runabout slides into the water from one of the simplest types of trailers—a single fixed support frame mounted on two wheels. The trailer is backed into the water allowing the boat to be pushed on or floated off. Many trailers are more sophisticated and incorporate tilt-up frames for launching.

Securely mounted on its four-wheeled trailer, a compact outboard cruiser moves down a highway on Long Island. State regulations specify the kind of hitch employed to attach the trailer to the car and require brake and signal lights, as well as safety chains on the hitch. A typical limit on the beam of the boat itself is 8 feet, and a 55-foot limit is usually set for the combined length of trailer and car.

A No-Frills Boat Club

Located on Keystone Reservoir near Tulsa, Oklahoma, the Windycrest Sailing Club typifies the new boat associations that take up where oldtime yacht clubs leave off. Although the club was founded in 1966, its members did not get around to building a clubhouse (center) until 1974, giving priority to the more vital approach road, parking lot and launching ramp—all constructed by the members themselves. Most of Windycrest's sailors use their boats only on weekends. Weekdays, many boats are pulled from the water and left on their trailers.

A Traditional Yacht Club

The gleaming club launch taxiing an owner to his Larchmont Yacht Club mooring on Long Island Sound in New York suggests the kind of cosseting members of established yacht clubs get for their money—in Larchmont's case almost $1,000 in annual dues. Along with a protected anchorage and the services of a launch, members can also use the club's handsome dining room and bar, fly the club's flag and enjoy reciprocal guest privileges at other clubs. For all their soaring costs, most old-line yacht clubs have long waiting lists of applicants.

The Ultimate Marina

California's Marina del Rey, three and a half miles southeast of Santa Monica harbor, is probably the ultimate in man-made boat basins. Besides its thousands of boat slips and handy access to nearby swimming pools and tennis courts, this marina complex offers ship's hardware stores, shipbuilder's lumberyards, ironworks, boatyards and boatbuilders. Dock space is usually available for overnight transients, along with an anchorage area in case the slips are full. Like most such facilities, Marina del Rey bases its charges on the length of the boat and on whether or not the owner lives aboard.

In a dredged salt marsh that was once the haunt of duck hunters, the futuristic Marina del Rey covers well over 500 acres and berths almost 6,000 boats. Six years in the building, at a cost of $32 million, it opened for business in 1965 and has been chock full ever since.

Glossary

Abaft Toward the rear of the boat relative to a point of reference; e.g., the mizzenmast is abaft the mainmast.

Abeam A direction off the boat at right angles to the fore-and-aft line amidships.

Aft Toward the stern.

Amidships In or near the middle of the boat, either along the longitudinal axis or from side to side.

Astern Behind the boat.

Athwartships Across the boat.

Ballast Weight, usually iron or lead, carried inside the boat or outside on the keel for trim or for stability.

Beam The width of the boat at its widest part. A boat is "on her beam ends" when heeled over 90°.

Beat To go to windward in a sailboat by sailing with the wind first on one side and then on the other.

Belay To secure a line, usually to a cleat.

Berth Space allotted to a boat at a dock, mooring area or anchorage. To give a wide berth is to give plenty of room. Also, a place to sleep on a boat, a bunk.

Bilge Area, usually beneath floorboards, inside the hull near the bottom.

Binnacle Housing of the compass.

Block A wood or metal shell that encloses one or more sheaves, or pulleys, through which lines are led.

Boat Any small craft propelled by oars, sails or engine.

Boom A projecting spar used to hold down and extend the foot of a sail.

Bow The forward part of the boat. (The word prow, cherished by poets, describes a ship's ornamented stem and is otherwise avoided by seamen.)

Bulkhead Any wall in a boat.

Cabin The enclosed area belowdecks.

Cabin trunk A structure built up above the deck and providing headroom below.

Caulking The waterproofing compound packed into the seams of a planked boat to make it watertight.

Centerboard A plate of wood or metal, hinged on a pin and lowered into the water through a watertight housing, or trunk. A centerboard resists the tendency of a sailboat to slide sideways when sailing.

Chain plate A long, narrow metal plate attached to the side of the hull as a fastening point for shrouds and stays.

Chine A sharp-angled intersection between a boat's topsides and bottom.

Chock A metal fitting, usually mounted on or in a boat's rail, to guide hawsers or ropes for mooring or towing.

Cleat A wood or metal fitting with two projecting horns—fastened to a boat's deck, mast or coaming—to which a line is belayed.

Coaming A raised framing around deck openings such as hatches or cockpits to keep water out.

Cockpit A well in the deck, usually aft, where a boat's wheel or tiller is located.

Companionway A passageway through which a ladder or stairs lead from the deck down to the cabin.

Counter The underside of the overhanging part of the stern above the waterline.

Cuddy A small, enclosed space or cabin in a small boat.

Cutter A sailboat with one mast stepped more than one third of the way aft, usually carrying two or more sails ahead of the mast. Also, a Coast Guard vessel.

Daggerboard A removable centerboard with no pivot pin.

Deadrise The angle at which the bottom rises from where it joins the keel to the turn of the bilge, or chine.

Deck What a floor is to a house.

Displacement The weight of water displaced by a floating boat, equal to the weight of the boat.

Dorade ventilator A deck box with cowl and internal arrangement that allows air but not water to enter the cabin.

Draft The depth a vessel extends below the waterline. A boat is said to draw so much water.

Dry rot Decay of wood caused by a fungus that flourishes in a moist, unventilated environment.

Fair Smooth, unfouled, favorable, as a fair hull or a fair wind.

Fend off To prevent a moving boat from hitting a dock or other object.

Fiberglass A cloth, mat or roving of glass fibers laminated with plastic resin; used extensively in boat construction.

Flare Outward spread and upward curve of the topsides as they rise from the waterline, most noticeably in the bow sections. The final, most pronounced curve of flare is called flam.

Flying bridge A raised platform that affords unobstructed vision for steering and navigation.

Foot Bottom edge of a sail.

Fore and aft A boat's longitudinal axis.

Forestay A supporting stay leading from the mast forward, aft of the headstay.

Foretriangle On a sailboat, the triangle formed by the headstay, the front of the mast and the deck.

Forward In or toward the bow.

Fractional rig A rig in which the headstay meets the mast at some distance below the masthead.

Freeboard Distance between the actual waterline of a boat and its rail.

Gaff A spar to support and spread the head of a sail of four generally unequal sides. A sail so rigged is gaff-headed.

Galley A seagoing kitchen.

Garboard The first plank, or strake, out from the keel.

Gear A general term for any collection of equipment, clothing or tools; e.g., oilskins and boots are foul-weather gear.

Gel coat The thin, outer coat of a fiberglass hull, often impregnated with color.

Genoa jib A large headsail set on the headstay and overlapping the mainsail.

Gunwale The rail of a boat. (Pronounced GUN-nel.)

Halyard A line to hoist and lower a sail.

Hatch An opening in the deck giving access below; also its cover.

Hawser A heavy line or cable, five inches or more in circumference, used on ships for mooring or towing.

Head The top corner of a triangular sail. Also, a seagoing lavatory.

Headsails Sails set within the foretriangle, i.e., forward of the mast and usually on a stay. Headsails include jibs and staysails.

Headstay Foremost stay supporting the mast. The jib is set on the headstay.

Heel A sideways leaning of a boat caused by the wind's force on the sails. Boats that heel easily are called tender or cranky; those that resist heeling are stiff.

Helm The device, usually a tiller or wheel, attached or connected to the rudder by which a boat is steered.

Hull The basic structural shell of a boat.

Hull speed The limit of speed imposed on a displacement hull by the resistance of its own wave systems.

Inboard Toward a boat's centerline. Also, a common contraction for a boat with an inboard engine.

Inboard engine An engine permanently mounted inside a boat's hull.

Jib A triangular sail set on the headstay.

Jib-headed A triangular sail supported by a halyard directly attached to its head—as opposed to a sail that is gaff-headed.

Jigger Common alternate name for the sail set on the mizzenmast.

Keel A main structural member, the backbone of the ship running longitudinally along the bottom from stem to stern. Also, the vertical downward extension of a sailboat's bottom, usually ballasted, for stability and lateral resistance.

Ketch A boat with a two-masted rig in which the larger, or mainmast, is forward, and the smaller mizzenmast is stepped aft—but forward of the rudder and, usually, of the helm.

Knot A fastening made with rope. Also, a unit measure of speed: one knot equals one nautical mile per hour. Since a nautical mile is about 800 feet longer than a land mile, a knot equals 1.15 mph.

Lazarette A stowage space in the stern.

Leech The after edge of a sail.

Leeward In the direction away from the wind. (Pronounced LOO-ard.)

Leeway Drift, or sideways slip, of a boat due to the pressure of wind on the sails.

Length The greatest length of a boat, not counting the bowsprit or other protuberances, is called length overall (LOA). Waterline length (LWL), usually shorter, is measured at the designed waterline and excludes the bow and stern overhangs.

Life lines Safety lines and guard rails rigged around a boat's deck to prevent the crew from being washed overboard.

Line Nautical usage for rope used aboard a boat.

List A hull's more or less permanent leaning to one side due to improper distribution of ballast or to taking water aboard.

Locker A chest, cupboard or small compartment for stowing gear.

Lower unit The drive shaft, gearing and propeller of an outboard motor.

Luff The leading edge of a sail. To luff up is to head a boat so close to the wind that the sails begin to flutter.

Mainmast Usually the principal and heaviest mast of two or more. In yawls and ketches the forward mast is the mainmast, in schooners and vessels with more than two masts, it is the second from forward.

Mainsail The sail set on the after side of the mainmast, usually the biggest working sail. Often called simply the main.

Mainsheet The line used to pull in and let out the mainsail.

Marconi Name to describe a three-cor-

nered sail whose luff sets on a mast—as opposed to the four-sided gaff-rigged sail. Also called a Bermuda or jib-headed sail.

Mast A wood or metal spar, stepped on the top of the structural keel or on the deck, that supports the booms, gaffs, yards and gear for spreading sail. The mast is held up by the standing rigging.

Mast step Socket in which the heel, or bottom, of the mast is stepped.

Masthead rig A rig in which the jib and spinnaker hoist to the top of the mast instead of partway down, as in a fractional rig.

Mizzen The sail set on the after side of the mizzenmast.

Mizzenmast Aftermast on a yawl or ketch.

Mooring A fixed anchor or weight by which a boat is kept at a permanent berth.

Outboard Out from the hull, or toward the outside, away from the centerline. Also, a contraction for outboard motor.

Outboard motor An engine mounted with clamps outside a boat's hull.

Overboard Over the side.

Overhead What a ceiling is to a house.

Planking Collectively, the planks of a wood hull attached to frames, or ribs.

Point To sail close to the wind. Also, one of 32 divisions on the compass, each equal to 11¼°.

Port The left side of the boat, looking forward. Also, a contraction for porthole.

Porthole A small, usually round opening or window in topsides or cabin trunk.

Pulpit A strong railing mounted at the bow or stern of ocean-racing sailboats to prevent crew members from going overboard. Also, a railed platform extending forward from the bow of a sport fisherman, used as a vantage point for sighting, spearing or gaffing fish.

Quarter Either side of a boat's stern.

Reach A course sailed between a beat and a run, with the wind coming more or less at right angles over the boat's side. In a close reach the wind is farther forward; in a broad reach, farther aft.

Rig A noun indicating the arrangement of masts, rigging and sails by which a vessel is distinguished, as a ketch or a yawl, etc. Also, a verb meaning to prepare a boat or some piece of nautical gear for service.

Rigging The lines or wires fitted to spars and sails for support and control. Standing rigging is made up of the fixed shrouds and stays that provide lateral and longitudinal support to the spars. Running rigging comprises the halyards, sheets, tackles, outhauls and downhauls to put up, take down and adjust sail.

Rope Cordage with fiber or wire strands twisted or braided. Rope used aboard a boat is called a line—with a few traditional exceptions, such as a bucket rope or bell rope.

Rudder A flat vertical piece extending from the hull, aft, by which the vessel is steered.

Run To sail before the wind. Also the narrowing part of the hull, aft, below the water.

Running lights Navigation lights required by rules of the nautical road in different combinations for different sizes and types of vessel. Usually they consist of a red light to port and green to starboard, plus one or more white lights.

Sail A piece of fabric rigged onto a spar or a stay to extract energy from the wind.

Schooner A sailboat that generally has two masts (though some have had up to seven); the mainmast is aft of a smaller foremast, and the sails are either jib-headed or gaff-headed.

Scupper A hole or opening in a rail, hatch or ventilator, to allow water to drain off.

Seacock An on-off valve attached to the through-hull pipes.

Shaft Transmits engine rotation to the propeller.

Sheave The grooved wheel (or roller or pulley) in a block over which a rope runs. (Pronounced shiv.)

Sheer The curve of a boat's rail from stem to stern.

Sheet A line attached to the clew of a sail or boom by which the sail is controlled.

Shrouds Ropes or wires, usually in pairs, led from the mast to chain plates at deck level on either side of the mast to keep it from falling sideways.

Sloop A sailboat with a single mast that is stepped not more than one third of the way aft from the bow. A sloop usually carries only one headsail.

Spar General term for any wood or metal pole—mast, boom, yard, gaff or sprit—used to carry and give shape to sails.

Spinnaker A full-bellied, lightweight sail set on a spinnaker pole and carried when a sailboat is reaching or running.

Spreaders Pairs of horizontal struts attached to each side of the mast and used to hold the shrouds away from the mast, thus giving them a wider purchase.

Starboard The right side of the boat, facing forward.

Stay A rope or wire running forward or aft from the mast to support it.

Stem The forwardmost part of the bow.

Stern The rear, or after, part of the boat.

Stern drive A system of power propulsion in which an inboard engine drives a propeller unit that resembles the lower unit of an outboard in appearance and function. Sometimes called inboard/outboard, or I/O.

Storm jib A small, strong jib used in heavy weather. Colloquially called a spitfire.

Strake A row of planking or plating running the length of a hull, identified by name as the sheer strake, the hull's topmost plank or the garboard strake, next to the keel.

Stuffing box A fitting around a moving part, such as the propeller or rudder shaft, that is located where the moving part goes through the hull. A stuffing box contains oiled packing, compressed by a packing gland, to lubricate the shaft's movement and also to seal the through-hull passage from water.

Tack A noun indicating the lower forward corner of a sail. Also, as a verb, to alter a boat's course through the eye of the wind so that the wind blows on the other side of the boat. A vessel is on port tack if the wind comes over the port side.

Thwart A crosswise seat in a small open boat.

Tiller An arm, or lever, connected to the rudder for steering.

Topside On deck.

Topsides The sides of the boat from waterline to rail.

Transom The aftermost part of the stern, which usually carries a boat's name, generally surmounting the counter.

Trim To adjust a boat's load so that the craft rides at the desired attitude. Also, to adjust the sheet controlling a sail.

Tumble home Inclination inward of vessel's sides from waterline to deck.

Turn of the bilge The curve where the bottom of a boat meets the topsides.

Turnbuckle An adjustable fastening for attaching the standing rigging to the chain plates.

Waterline The actual level of the water on a floating hull; a painted line marking the designed waterline is called a boot top.

Wetted surface The immersed area of a floating hull including keel and rudder.

Winch A machine around which a line is turned to provide mechanical advantage for hoisting or hauling.

Windward The direction toward the wind source.

Working sails Those normally used in moderate weather—as opposed to light, storm or racing sails.

Yawl A boat with a two-masted rig in which the mizzen, or jigger, is abaft the rudderpost and the helm; the yawl's mizzen is smaller than the ketch's, as well as being placed farther aft.

Bibliography

General

Calahan, H. A., *So You're Going to Buy a Boat*. The Macmillan Company, 1947.

Chapman, Charles F., *Piloting, Seamanship & Small Boat Handling*. Motor Boating & Sailing, 1972.

Cozzens, Fred S., *American Yachts and Yachting*. Cassell & Company, Ltd., 1887.

de Kerchove, René, *International Maritime Dictionary*. D. Van Nostrand Company, Inc., 1961.

Duffett, John, *Modern Marine Maintenance*. Motor Boating & Sailing Books, 1973.

Gilfillan, S. C., Ph.D., *Inventing the Ship*. Follett Publishing Company, 1935.

Heaton, Peter:
The Yachtsman's Vade Mecum. Adam & Charles Black, 1969.
Yachting, A Pictorial History. The Viking Press, 1972.

Henderson, Richard, *The Cruiser's Compendium*. Henry Regnery Co., 1973.

Henderson, Richard, with Bartlett S. Dunbar, *Sail and Power*. Naval Institute Press, 1973.

Herreshoff, L. Francis, *Capt. Nat Herreshoff, The Wizard of Bristol*. Sheridan House, 1953.

Illingworth, J. H., *Further Offshore*. Quadrangle Books, 1969.

Lane, Carl D., *The New Boatman's Manual*. W. W. Norton & Company, Inc., 1962.

Lewis, Leland R., and Peter Eric Ebeling, *Sea Guide*, Vol. I. Sea Publications Inc., 1973.

Manry, Robert, *Tinkerbelle*. Harper and Row, 1966.

McEwen, W. A., and A. H. Lewis, *Encyclopedia of Nautical Knowledge*. Cornell Maritime Press, 1953.

Mitchell, Carleton, *The Winds Call*. Charles Scribner's Sons, 1971.

One-Design & Offshore Yachtsman, eds., *Encyclopedia of Sailing*. Harper and Row, 1971.

Phillips-Birt, D., *Yachting World Handbook*. St. Martins Press, 1967.

Robinson, Bill:
Legendary Yachts. The Macmillan Company, 1971.
The World of Yachting. Random House, 1966.

Sleightholme, J. D., *A B C For Yachtsmen*. Adlard Coles Ltd., 1965.

Stephens, W. P., *American Yachting*. The Macmillan Company, 1904.

Taylor, William H., and Stanley Rosenfeld, *The Story of American Yachting*.

Appleton-Century-Crofts, Inc., 1958.

Weeks, Morris, Jr., ed., *The Complete Boating Encyclopedia*. Golden Press, 1964.

Zadig, Ernest A., *The Complete Book of Boating*. Prentice Hall, 1972.

Construction and Design

Benford, Jay R., and Herman Husen, *Practical Ferro-Cement Boatbuilding*. International Marine Publishing Company, 1971.

Bingham, Bruce, *Ferro-cement: design, techniques, and application*. Cornell Maritime Press, Inc., 1974.

Brewer, Edward S., and Jim Betts, *Understanding Boat Design*. International Marine Publishing Company, 1971.

Cobb, Boughton Jr., *Fiberglass Boats, Construction and Maintenance*. Yachting Publishing Corporation, 1973.

Herreshoff, L. Francis, *The Common Sense of Yacht Design*. Caravan-Maritime Books, 1973.

Kinney, Francis S., *Skene's Elements of Yacht Design*. Dodd, Mead & Company, 1962.

Phillips-Birt, Douglas, *Sailing Yacht Design*. International Marine Publishing Company, 1971.

Simpson, Tracy W., *Aluminum Boats*. Kaiser Aluminum and Chemical Sales, Inc., 1964.

Steward, Robert M., *Boatbuilding Manual*. International Marine Publishing Company, 1970.

Zadig, Ernest A., *The Boatman's Guide to Modern Marine Materials*. Motor Boating & Sailing Books, 1974.

Sailing

Baader, Juan, *The Sailing Yacht*. W. W. Norton & Company, Inc., 1965.

Coles, K. Adlard, *Heavy Weather Sailing*. First American Printing. John de Graff Inc., 1968.

Cotter, Edward F., *Multihull Sailboats*. Crown Publishers, 1971.

Howard-Williams, Jeremy, *Sails*. John de Graff, Inc., 1972.

Kay, H. F., *The science of yachts, wind & water*. John de Graff, Inc., 1971.

Street, Donald M., Jr., *The Ocean Sailing Yacht*. W. W. Norton & Company, Inc., 1973.

Power Boating

Anderson, Edwin P., *Audels Outboard Motor and Boating Guide*. Theo. Audel & Co., 1962.

Bowman, Hank Wieand, *The Encyclopedia of Outboard Motorboating*. A. S. Barnes & Company, 1955.

Chilton's Repair and Tune-Up Guide: *Outboard Motors Under 30 Horsepower*. Chilton Book Company, 1973.
Outboard Motors 30 Horsepower and Over. Chilton Book Company, 1973.

Miller, Conrad, *Small Boat Engines, Inboard and Outboard*. Sheridan House, 1970.

Nabb, Edward H., *Care and Repair of Your Inboard Engine*. Chilton Book Company, 1961.

Warren, Nigel, *Marine Conversions*. Adlard Coles Limited, 1972.

West, Jack, *Modern Powerboats*. Van Nostrand Reinhold Company, 1970.

Witt, Glen L., *Inboard Motor Installations in Small Boats*. Glenn, 1960.

Boating Courses

A prudent step between reading about boating and going afloat is taking a course in boat handling, seamanship and safety. Hundreds of local schools and clubs schedule private classes in all facets of boating. The national organizations listed below provide curricula free or at little cost. Many state and city recreation departments also sponsor public courses.

1. U.S. Power Squadrons. More than 400 local units of this national organization of recreational boatmen present free to the public a 10-lesson course in basic boating safety at least once a year. To its members, the USPS also offers advanced instruction on seamanship and navigation. For information, call your local unit, or national headquarters in Mondale, New Jersey, toll free, (800) 243-6000.

2. The U.S. Coast Guard. For those who live where other general courses are unavailable, the Coast Guard offers a correspondence "Skipper's Course." Write to the Office of Boating Safety, 400 Seventh Street, SW, Washington, D.C. 20590.

3. The Coast Guard Auxiliary. A volunteer civilian arm of the service, the auxiliary sponsors a number of courses in boating safety for the public. Call one of the 18 district offices or your local group.

4. The American Red Cross. Many local Red Cross chapters periodically conduct small-boat safety classes designed by the national organization.

Acknowledgments

Portions of *The Boat* were written by Reginald Bragonier Jr., Roger Hamilton, Peter Swerdloff and Keith Wheeler. For help given in the preparation of this book the editors also wish to thank the following: Henry H. Anderson Jr., New York, New York; Ralph Ainuzzi, H. A. Bruno and Associates, Inc., New York, New York; Jake and Martha Bauer, Ferro-Boat Builders, Inc., Edgewater, Maryland; Robert R. Boulware, Assistant Coordinator of Public Affairs, Mystic Seaport, Mystic, Connecticut; Grace Brynolson, New York, New York; Dennis Dobson, Glastron Boat Company, Austin, Texas; Otto Doll, Yacht Haven, Stamford, Connecticut; Jules Fleder, Director of Westlawn School of Yacht Design, National Association of Engine and Boat Manufacturers, Greenwich, Connecticut; George R. Hinman, Port Washington, New York; Sohei Hohri, Librarian, New York Yacht Club, New York, New York; Carol Karnatz, Minnesota Historical Society, St. Paul, Minnesota; Robert Kress, Michigan Wheel Co., Grand Rapids, Michigan; William S. Luckett, Vice Commodore, Larchmont Yacht Club, Larchmont, New York; Howard McMichaels Jr., McMichaels' Boats, Mamaroneck, New York; Ted Martin, Bellevue, Washington; William D. Munro, Upper Montclair, New Jersey; Ian Nicholls, Barient Winch Co., Darien, Connecticut; Don O'Keefe, Derecktor's Yacht Yard, Mamaroneck, New York; John H. Page, Huntington, New York; Charles Pigadis, President, Lakes Yacht Sales, Inc., Freeport, New York; Sydney H. Rogers, Publisher, *Boating*, New York, New York; Robert F. Smith, Lehman Manufacturing Co., Linden, New Jersey; Peter A. Sturcke, Vice President, Sen Dure Products, Inc., Bay Shore, New York; John Wilhelm, Los Angeles, California.

Picture Credits

Credits from left to right are separated by semicolons, from top to bottom by dashes.

Cover—John Zimmerman. 6,7—Tom Sawyer. 9—Sebastian Milito. 10—Morris Rosenfeld. 11—Sebastian Milito. 12—John Zimmerman. 14,15—Stephen Green-Armytage; Tom McCarthy—Scott Ransom. 16,17—Chris Caswell; Paul A. Darling. 18—Tom McCarthy—Stanley Rosenfeld. 19—Enrico Ferorelli. 20,21—Eric Schweikardt for SPORTS ILLUSTRATED. 22—Tom McCarthy. 23—Eric Schweikardt for SPORTS ILLUSTRATED. 24,25—Lynn Pelham; Mercury Marine—Gary E. Miller. 26,27—George Silk. 28—Paul A. Darling. 29—Richard Meek for SPORTS ILLUSTRATED. 30,31—Tom McCarthy. 32—Drawings courtesy *Yachting World*. 34 through 57—Drawings by William G. Teodecki. 58—The Bettmann Archive. 59—Alice Austen, courtesy Staten Island Historical Society. 60,61—Photography Collection, Suzzallo Library, University of Washington; Minnesota Historical Society. 62,63—H. H. Bennett Studio; Irving Brown Collection, The State Historical Society of Wisconsin—Minnesota Historical Society. 64,65—The Bancroft Library, except top left courtesy Minneapolis Public Library. 66,67—Bish Collection, The State Historical Society of Wisconsin, WH1(B5)281; Library of Congress. 68,69—Minnesota Historical Society; L. C. McClure, courtesy Western History Department, Denver Public Library. 70—Richard Meek. 74 through 79—Carl Mydans. 80,81—Arthur Rickerby, from TIME-LIFE Picture Agency; Richard Meek (2). 82 through 85—Bill Eppridge. 86 through 91—Richard Meek. 92—Tom Sawyer. 94 through 113—Drawings by Roger Metcalf. 103—top adapted from Stanley Rosenfeld photo—bottom adapted from John Smallman photo. 114—Richard Meek for SPORTS ILLUSTRATED. 116 through 127—Drawings by Nicholas Fasciano. 128 through 131—Eric Schweikardt for SPORTS ILLUSTRATED. 132—Enrico Ferorelli. 134 through 144—Stanley Rosenfeld. 145—Stanley Rosenfeld; Enrico Ferorelli. 148 through 151—George Silk except far left on 150 Bill Eppridge. 152,153—Bill Eppridge. 154—George Silk. 156—David A. Bast. 158,159—Al Freni. 160,161—Jim Olive. 162,163—Al Freni. 164 through 167—John Zimmerman.

Index
Numerals in italics indicate a photograph or drawing of the subject mentioned.

Accommodations, 114, 115, *118, 119, 122, 123, 125, 127*
Adze, *75*
Aerodynamic forces in sailing, *92, 93, 94-97, 103*
Air pressure, *94, 95*
Airfoils, *93, 94-97, 103*
Alternator, *104*
Aluminum: alloys, 72; comparison with other materials, 73; construction, *70, 71-73, 86-91*; problems, 140, *141*; survey, 146
Ark, 44
Atkin, John, *132,* 133

Backstay, *98, 99*
Ballast, *54-56;* survey, 146
Battery charging, *120. See* Alternator
Beam, *34,* 54
Beat, *92, 94, 95, 96*
Bernoulli, Daniel, 95
Bernoulli's law, 95
Berths: bunk, *118, 119, 122, 123, 125, 127,* boat, 157
Bicycle skiff, *64*
Bilge, 36, *37;* turn of the bilge, 37, *135*
Bilge boards, *52*
Bilge pump, *122, 123*
Binnacle, *116*
Blackfin, 29
Blowers, 120
Board boats, 52, 100; Laser, 52; Sunfish, 13, *17, 52, 160*
Boat clubs, 157, *160, 161*
Boat shows, 148, *149-154*
Bonanza, 39, 128-131
Bows, 34, *35, 38, 39*
Buying a boat, 133-155

Cabin cruiser, *24, 35, 120-123, 132*
Canoe: aluminum, *14, 15*; dugout, *47*; outrigger, *18*; sailing, 58, *64*
Caribbee, 11
Catamarans, *96, 103*; sailing, *18, 53*
Catboat, *59, 100*
Cathedral hull, *45, 113*
Caulking, *79, 135,* 146
Cavitation, 108, *109*
Center of buoyancy, *54, 55*
Center of gravity, *54, 55*
Centerboard, *36, 50, 51*; centerboard trunk, *51*; survey, 146
Centerboard hull, *50, 51*
Chain locker, *120*
Chain plates, *98, 99*
Character boats, *22, 23*
Chine, *36, 37*
Choosing a boat, 12-31; big powerboats, *24, 25*; big sailboats, *28, 29*; canoes and rowboats, *14, 15*; character boats, *22, 23*; custom boats, *26, 27*; houseboats, *30, 31*; powerboats, *20,*

21; racing sailboats, *18, 19*; small sailboats, *16, 17*
Clear Lake Sailing Club, *157*
Cleopatra's Barge, 58
Clipper bow, *38*
Clutch, *106*
Coast Guard, 104
Cockpit, 34; lockers, *116*; power, *123-125*; sail, *116, 126, 127*
Companionway, *34, 116*
Compass position, *116*
Construction, 70-91; aluminum, *70,71-73, 86-91*; ferro-cement, *71-73, 80, 81*; fiberglass, *71-73, 82-85*; steel, *71, 73*; wood, *71, 73, 74-79*
Control panel, *120, 124, 125*; center console, *124, 125*
Controls, auxiliary engine, *116*
Corrosion, *72, 73, 140, 141, 142, 144*
Costs of ownership, 154-155
Counter, *35, 39*
Crossbow, proa, *57*
Crowninshield, George, 58
Cruising boats, *24, 25, 28, 116-119, 120, 123, 125, 127*
Cutter, *100*

Daysailer, *127*
Deadrise, 36, *37, 44*
Deck covering, *145*
Deck hardware, *116, 117, 120, 121, 124-127,* survey, 146
Deep-V hull, *44, 113*
Delamination, *137*
Dhow, *100*
Diesel engines, 93, 106
Dinette, 115, *122, 123*
Displacement, *34, 35*
Displacement hulls, 34, *46, 51*
Dorade, 117
Dorade ventilator, *117*
Doubloon, 116
Draft, *34*
Drag, *40, 41, 95*
Drive system, *106, 107*
Drop keel, *50*
Dry rot, *136, 137;* survey, 146, 147

Electric paddlewheeler, *67*
Electrical system, 120, 123; survey, 147
Engine, *93;* auxiliary, *116, 118, 119;* cooling, *104, 105;* diesel, 93, 106; gasoline, 93, 104-106; inboard, *93, 104-107;* internal combustion, 93, 104; outboard, *13, 93, 110-112,* 113, *124, 125;* steam, 58, 66, 93; two-cycle, *110, 111-113;* water pump, *104*
Engine compartment, *115,* 120, *121*
Engine controls, *120, 121*
Engine problems, *142, 143;* survey, 147
Equilibrium, 95

Fastenings, *134, 135, 138,* 142, *144;* survey, 146, 147
Ferro-cement: comparison with other materials, 73; construction, *71-73, 80, 81;* problems, *140;* survey, 146
Fiberglass: comparison with other materials, 73; construction, *71-73, 82-85;* mat, *82;* problems, *138, 139;* roving, *82;* survey, 139, 146, 147
Fin keel, *49*
Finisterre, 10, 114, 115
Finn, 52
Flame arrester, 104, *105*
Flare, *36, 37, 46*
Flat bottom, *42,* 113
Flying bridge, *120, 121*
Flying Dutchman, 52
Flying Junior, *16*
Flywheel, *106*
Forefoot, *35*
470, 52
Frames, *74, 77*
Freeboard, *35*

Gaff rigs, *100, 101*
Galley, 115, *118,* 119, *122,* 123
Gasoline engines: inboard, *93, 104, 105,* 106, *107*; inboard-outboard, 73, *112;* outboard, *93,* 110, *111-113*
Gel coat, 73, *82,* 139; survey, 146
Genoa, 96, *97-103*
Gimbals, 115, *119*
Gloriana, 48
Grab rail, 34, *116, 117, 120*
Grand Lake, Colo., *68, 69*

Half Moon, 44
Halyards, 99, 116, *117*
Hardware, *116, 117;* survey, 146
Hatch, 116, 117, *120, 121*
Head, *122, 123*
Headsails, *96-103*
Headstay, *98, 99*
Heat exchanger, 104, *105*
Heel, *54-57*
Herreshoff, Nathaniel, 33, 48
Hiking out, *56, 127*
Hogging, 135, 146
Holding tank, *123*
Houseboats, *30, 31, 42,* 113
Hull, 33-57; structural problems, *134, 135, 138, 140;* survey, 146
Hull form: cathedral, 44, *45;* centerboard, *51;* centerboard keel, *50;* deep-V, *44;* displacement, *46;* fin keel, *49;* flat bottom, *42;* full keel, *48;* semidisplacement, *45;* semi-V, *43*
Hull contours and profiles, *36, 37*
Hull design, 32-57
Hull shapes, *42-53*
Hull speed, 40
Hunt, Ray, 44

Hydrodynamics, 33, 40, 41, *95*

Inboard-outboard, *112*, 113, 124, 125; problems, *142, 143*
Insurance, 155
Interiors, *114*, 115, *118, 119*, 122, 123, 125, *127-131*; galley, *118, 119*, 122, 123; guest stateroom, 130; head, *122*, 123

Jet drive, 106, *107*
Jib, 96; flying jib, *101*; genoa, *97-103*; working, 96, *100-102*
Jib and jigger, *102*
Jumper struts, *98*

Kayak, 15, 47, 58
Keel, *36*, 71, *75-77, 95*; fin, *49*; full, *48*; lead ballast, *87*; problems, *138*
Keel bolts, *134, 135*; survey, 146
Keel centerboarder, *50*
Ketch, *101, 103*
Knuckle bow, *39*

Lands End, 9, *11*
Lapstrake construction, *63*
Larchmont Yacht Club, *162, 163*
Laser, 52
Lateen sail, *100*
Lateral force, *94-97*; as stress, *98*
Launch service, *162, 163*
Lazarette, *144*
Leaks, *134, 135*; survey, 146, 147
Length: overall (LOA), *34*; waterline (LWL), *34*
Life lines, 115, *116, 117*; survey, 146

MacGregor, John, 58
Mainsail, *94-103*
Maintenance, 73; costs, 155
Manry, Robert, 127
Marconi, Guglielmo, 100
Marconi rig, *98-103*
Marina, *164-167*
Marina del Rey, *164-167*
Mariner, 86-91
Masthead rig, *98, 99*
Masts, *98, 99*; damage, *145*; survey, 147
Measurement: beam, *34*; draft, *34*; freeboard, *35*; length, *34*; topsides, *35*
Merrimac, 86
Mini-craft scooters, *22*
Miss Nylex, 103
Mitchell, Carleton, 8-11
Mizzen, *101-103*
Monitor, 86
Mooring, *156, 157, 163*
Moppie, 44
Multihulls, *53*

Naphtha, 58
Nervi, Luigi, 71
New York Yacht Club, 58, 65
Noah, 115

Olympic classes: Flying Dutchman, 52; Finn, 52; Tempest, *18*, 52
Ondine, 103
One-design boats, 51; A-class scow, 52; E-class scow, 18, *19*; M-class scow, 52; Finn, 52; Flying Junior, *16, 17*; Flying Dutchman, 52; 470, 52; Laser, 52; Star, 49; Sunfish, 13, *17*, 52, *160*; Tempest, *18*, 52
Outboard motors, 13, 93, *110-112*, 113, *124, 125*
Outrigger canoe, 18, 57
Ownership costs, 155

Paddle wheel, 67
Planing hull, 34, 40, *41-46*; sail, *52*
Planking, 74, 79, *134, 135*; survey, 146
Plumb bow, 38
Plumbing survey, 147
Plywood, 72, 73; delamination, *137*; survey, 146
Points of sailing: beating, 92, *94, 96*; reaching, 97; running, 97
Powerboat: choice of, 13, *20-27*, 30, 31; cockpit arrangements, *123-125*; control systems, 120, *121*; sterns, *38, 39*
Power train, 106, *107*
Pressure differential, *94, 95*
Proa, *57*
Propeller shaft, 107; problems, 143, 146
Propellers, 93, *108, 109*; folding, *109, 118*; pitch, diameter, *108*; problems, *142, 143*
Propulsion: power, 93, *104-112*, 113; sail, *92-103*; bicycle, *64*; electric, *67*; naphtha, 58; rowing, 15, *62, 63*; steam, 58, 66
Pulpit, 116, *117*
Pump: bilge, *122*; water, *104*

Racing sloop, *126*, 127
Reacher, *102*
Reaching, 96, 97, *102*
Reaching spinnaker, *102*
Reduction gear, *106*
Repairs, *134*
Resin, 72, 73, 82-84
Resistance: frictional, 40, *41, 95*; wave-making, *40*
Rig: fractional, *96-98*, 99; lateen, 100; masthead, *98-103*; split, 100
Rigging: failure, 99; running, 99; standing, *98, 99*; stresses, *98*; survey, 147
Righting arm, *54, 55, 57*
Rigs, basic, *100, 101*
Rowboats, 15, *62, 63*
Rudder, *34*; problems, *134*; survey, 146
Run, *34*
Runabout, *124*
Running, 96, 97
Running lights, 116, *117, 120, 121, 124, 125*

Rust, 73, *134, 141, 142*, 146

Sail plan, 100
Sailboats, trailerable, *50, 126, 127*
Sails: 93-103; battened, 96; fisherman's staysail, *102*; forestaysail, *100-102*; genoa, 96, *97-102*; headsails, *102*; jib, 96; lateen, *100*; main, 96; main staysail, *102*; mizzen, *101-103*; mizzen staysail, *102, 103*; parachute spinnaker, 97; reacher, *102*; reaching spinnaker, 102; spinnaker, 96, 97; spinnaker staysail, *102*; spitfire, *102*; staysails, *102*; storm jib, *102*; stormsails, *102*; storm trysail, *102*; survey, 147; topsail, *101*; wing sail, 103; working jib, 96, *102*; working sails, 96, 97
Sans Terre, 8, 9
Scarfing, 76
Schooner, 100, *101, 102*; staysail schooner, *102*
Scow, 18, *19*, 52, 68, 69
Scupper, 116, *117*
Seacock, 119, 123; survey, 147
Semidisplacement hull, *46*, 113
Semi-V, *43*, 113
Shear pin, *111*
Sheer, *38, 39*; raised deck, *39*; reverse, *39*; straight, *39*
Shore power connection, 120, 121, 123
Shrouds and stays, *98, 99, 117*; tension, 98, 135
Skeg, 36
Slocum, Captain Joshua, 119
Sloop, *100, 102*
Sloops, auxiliary cruising, *28*
Spars, *98, 99*
Spinnaker, 96, 97; parachute spinnaker as an airfoil, 97; reaching spinnaker, *102*; spinnaker staysail, *102*
Spitfire, *102*
Sport cruiser, *25*
Sport fisherman, *46, 124, 125*
Spray, 119
Spreaders, *98*
Square-stern canoe, *15*
Stability, *54-57*
Stanchions, 116, *117, 144*
Standing rigging, *98, 99*
Star, 49
Staysail schooner, *102*
Staysails: fisherman's, *102*; fore-, *101, 102*; main, *102*; mizzen, *102, 103*; spinnaker, *102*
Steam, 58, 66, 93
Steel construction, 73; problems, 140, *141*
Steering: cables, *121*; problems, *134, 142, 143*; survey, 147
Stem, *35*, 75, *135*
Stern, 34, *38, 39*; transom stern, *38*
Stern drive, *112*, 125; problems, *142, 143*
Storage, *158, 159*; rates, 155

Stormsails, *102*
Stove, alcohol, *119*
Strake, *44*
Stuffing box, 106, *107*
Sunfish, 13, *17, 52, 160*
Survey, 133-147; check list, 146-147
Surveyor, 133, 146

Teak, 71, 74
Tempest, *18, 52*
Thrust, 33; propeller, 93, 108, *109;* sail, *94-97;* as stress, *98*
Tiller, *34, 116, 126, 127*
Tinkerbelle, 127
Toerail, *116, 117, 120, 121*
Topside layout: power, *120, 121, 124, 125;* sail, *116, 117, 126, 127*
Topsides, *35, 37*
Towing, *40*
Trailers, 157, *158, 159;* launching, *158;* legal requirements, *159;* towing, *159*
Transmission, *106, 107*
Transoms, 34, *38;* reverse, *39;* separation problems, *139*
Trapeze, *56*

Traveler, *116, 126, 127*
Trawler, 47
Trawler yachts, *26, 27, 47, 72, 74-79*
Trimaran, *53*
Trysail, *102*
Tumble home, *37, 46*
Turn of the bilge, *36*
Turnbuckle, 99
12-meter racing sloops, *92, 93,* 99 aluminum, 70; construction, *86-91,* mast, 99

Unidilla, 66, 67
Universal joint, *107*
Used boats, 133-147

V-drive, 106, *107*
Ventilation, 115, 116, 137

Water scooter, *22*
Waterman, Cameron, 93
Welding, 86, *88, 90*
Wetted surface, *40, 41,* 95
Wheel steering, sail, 34, *116*
White Bear Lake, Minn., *60, 61, 68*

Winch, *116, 117,* 127, *144,* 146
Wind resistance, 99
Wind turbulence, *94,* 95
Windycrest Sailing Club, *160, 161*
Wing sail, *103*
Wisconsin Dells, Wis., *62, 63*
Wood construction, 71, 73, *74-79;* comparison with other materials, 73; problems, *134-137;* survey, 146, 147
Workboats, 58, *100*
Working sails, *96, 97, 100-103*

Yacht broker, 133
Yacht club, 157, *162, 163*
Yawl, *101, 102*

Printed in U.S.A.